Teen Violence

Look for these and other books in the Lucent Overview Series:

Teen Alcoholism
Teen Drug Abuse
Teen Pregnancy
Teen Prostitution
Teen Sexuality
Teen Suicide
Teen Violence

Teen
Violence

by William Goodwin

TEEN ISSUES

For Gideon and Marilyn,
making it through your teen years
loved, loving, unscathed, fortunate

Library of Congress Cataloging-in-Publication Data

Goodwin, William, 1943–
    Teen violence / by William Goodwin.
        p.   cm. — (Lucent overview series. Teen issues)
    Includes bibliographical references and index.
    Summary: An overview of violence by teenagers, examining its
causes, prevention, and handling by the juvenile justice system.
    ISBN 1-56006-511-7 (alk. paper)
    1. Juvenile delinquency—United States—Juvenile literature.
2. Violence—United States—Juvenile literature.   3. Juvenile
justice, Administration of—United States—Juvenile literature.
[1. Juvenile delinquency.   2. Violent crimes.   3. Justice, Administration of.]   I. Title.   II. Series.
HV9104.G634   1998
364.36'0973—dc21   97-37741
                                                                CIP
                                                                 AC

Copyright © 1998 by Lucent Books, Inc.
P.O. Box 289011, San Diego, CA 92198-9011
Printed in the U.S.A.

Contents

Introduction

STORIES OF VIOLENCE by and against youth explode from the news like gunshots from a passing car. It would seem that America is under attack by armed teenagers.

During the early 1980s, about a thousand murders were committed by teens each year in the United States. By the middle of the 1990s, that had grown to over three thousand per year, or almost 10 percent of all murders.

Numbers like that make it sound like teen violence is a growing epidemic, an impression that is given further validity by the Centers for Disease Control and Prevention in Atlanta, Georgia, which now identify teen violence as a major public health problem.

Talking about teen violence in terms of murder is the obvious thing to do because of the dramatic finality and loss that death brings, but the epidemic—if that is actually what it is—encompasses much more than murder. The statistics for armed robbery, assault, rape, and carjackings by juveniles in the United States are higher than in any other country in the world. The teenage perpetrators and victims come from every walk of life and every ethnic background. People of all ages are shocked, saddened, and frightened by this news, but no one is more immediately affected by the epidemic of teen violence than teenagers themselves.

Terminology of teen violence

Violence is any physical conduct that causes injury or harm to another person. Teen violence means that either the victim, the perpetrator, or both are between twelve and twenty years old. Teen violence includes murder, shooting, stabbing, beating, rape, robbery, and even simply threatening someone with physical harm. All are against the law.

The terms *teen*, *youth*, and *juvenile* are used more or less interchangeably when discussing violence by and against young people. A teen is a person between thirteen and twenty years old. Youth is a more general term applied to individuals between ages twelve and twenty-four. Juvenile has a precise meaning, especially to police and judges, since the Federal Bureau of Investigation (FBI) officially defines juvenile crime as illegal acts committed by persons ages ten through seventeen. Since statistics are not collected specifically for the teenagers, in this book most figures and examples are based on statistics for the juvenile group.

Young men are not the only perpetrators of teen violence. This young woman, for example, is a gang member in Los Angeles, California.

A new trend

The extent of teen violence seems overwhelming, yet there are rays of hope. Figures released by the FBI at the end of 1996 showed that in 1995, violent crime rates among juveniles dropped for the first time in seven years. Overall violent crime was down 4 percent for individuals under age seventeen, 7 percent among kids age ten to fourteen. Juvenile arrests specifically for murder also fell, 14 percent less than 1994 and 23 percent less than 1993. Furthermore, rape arrests among teens dropped 4 percent, robbery arrests dropped 1 percent, and aggravated assault arrests dropped 3 percent from 1994 to 1995. These declines were small, but they could be the start of a new trend—or they could be only a temporary downturn.

With most of the country expecting juvenile crime to continue growing, the 1995 statistics brought renewed hope to many people. U.S. attorney general Janet Reno was one of them. She stated that the figures proved that the "explosion in teenage crime can be averted through

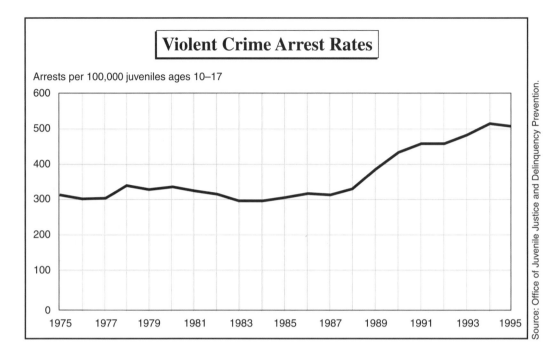

Violent Crime Arrest Rates

Arrests per 100,000 juveniles ages 10–17

Source: Office of Juvenile Justice and Delinquency Prevention.

community policing, mentor programs, and groups like the Boys and Girls Clubs. . . . We must do everything we can to prevent children from getting into trouble in the first place."

All the stories about teen violence in the news, however, tend to obscure the fact that the majority of young people are not involved in violent crimes as perpetrators or victims. Many civic leaders are anxious to put statistics on teen violence in perspective and leave the hysteria of the headlines behind. It seems people need to be reminded that teenagers are, as Hugh B. Price of the National Urban League said, "an asset to their communities and to this country, not a liability."

1

The Scope of Teen Violence

"REPORT FINDS SURGE IN HOMICIDAL TEENS" shrieks a 1992 headline in the *Chicago Tribune*.

"Big Shots: An Inside Look at the Deadly Love Affair Between America's Kids and Their Guns" reads a *Time* magazine cover story in August 1993.

"Armed Without a Conscience: Handguns Fuel Teen Violence" frets the bold writing in a 1996 series on juvenile crime in the *San Diego Union-Tribune*.

For years, newspapers, magazines, and television have flooded the public with so many stories like these that most people believe that teen violence is one of America's most serious crime problems, maybe *the* most serious.

Scary statistics

People find the extraordinary increases in lethal violence among youth, however, more alarming than the government statistics that show that violence has increased in all segments of the U.S. population in recent years. Fueling the fascination with teen violence are a host of scary statistics. For example, according to the U.S. surgeon general's office, murder rates among American males under nineteen years old are twenty times as high as most other industrialized countries. Furthermore, the average age of the perpetrators and victims of teen violence has continued to fall. Violence now poisons many schools as increasing numbers of students carry guns in their backpacks. Each day an average of fourteen American children under the age of nineteen die in homicides, suicides, or accidental shootings, and many more are injured.

From a high in the 1960s, violent juvenile crime rates actually dropped during the next twenty-five years. In 1987, according to FBI data, only 8.5 percent of violent crimes were committed by juveniles, down from 14 percent in the 1960s. Since 1987, however, the juvenile contribution to the country's violent crime problem has risen steadily until the mid-1990s, when juveniles accounted for almost 13 percent of the violent crimes committed in the United States. According to nationwide statistics collected by the FBI, in the mid-1990s one out of every eight people who committed a violent crime that was later solved turned out to be a juvenile. Of all persons arrested for murder in the United States, 17 percent were teenagers.

Seeking perspective in the statistics

To gain a more complete perspective, it is necessary to go beyond the headlines and the obvious fact that there are more instances of serious teen violence in the 1990s than in the 1980s. Between 1974 and 1983, all violent crime reported to the police in the United States increased by 30 percent. The FBI attributes that increase entirely to adults since during that period the numbers of juvenile violent offenses per year remained unchanged. During the next ten-year period, 1983 to 1992, violent crime increased 54 percent. This time adults were responsible for only 81 percent of the increase. Juvenile crime was up, accounting for 19 percent of the total increase in all violent crimes. Thus, even though their part in the growth of violent crime has increased, juveniles are not the major factor in violent crime trends.

The alarming fact is that 25 percent of the increase in the most serious violence between 1983 and 1992—murder, rape, and robbery—was attributed to juveniles. Though adults have continued to be responsible for the greatest part of the growth in violent crime during the years since 1992, the juvenile contribution to the violence has been greater than in the past.

Furthermore, juveniles are not only committing more violent crime, but they are also more frequently its victims. In 1992, for example, almost 25 percent of all violent crimes were committed against juveniles, yet juveniles accounted for only 10 percent of the total U.S. population over the age of twelve.

According to FBI estimates, over 3,000 juveniles have been arrested for homicide and about 130,000 juveniles have been arrested for other violent crimes each year since 1991. Compare those figures to the nearly 1 million twelve- to nineteen-year-old victims of violent crime during each of those years. Violent crime in which juveniles were the victims increased 23.4 percent from 1987 to 1992, while the juvenile population increased only 1 percent. One in every 13 juveniles was the victim of a violent crime in 1992, double the rate for twenty-five- to thirty-four-year-olds.

Teenagers are victims of violence more than any other age group.

The U.S. Department of Justice reports that teens are victimized by crimes of violence more than any other age group. On the average, people between the ages of twelve and nineteen are victims of approximately 2 million violent crimes every year, and the government believes less than half of the crimes that actually occur are reported.

About statistics

Statistics—numbers, polls, surveys—are valuable tools in any effort to understand what is really happening. It is also true, however, that statistics can be wrong, incomplete, misinterpreted, and misrepresented.

In the June 1988 *USA Today* article entitled "Executing Juveniles Is a Social Necessity," the head of the Washington Legal Foundation was quoted as saying, "Nearly 20,000 murders are committed by juveniles every year." Compare that figure with the FBI statistics for 1988 that show a total of 16,326 murders and manslaughters were reported in the United States. Of the approximately 15,000 persons arrested for those crimes, only 1,765 were juveniles. Even that figure was probably too high because, as studies show, juveniles tend to get in trouble in groups and a single crime often results in multiple arrests of teenagers. Was that "20,000" figure quoted in the national newspaper a misprint? Was it an intentional distortion of the truth to drum up support for a political position? Without more information, readers can only guess.

This is not to say that teen violence has not increased a significant amount—by all indications it most certainly has. Statistics, however, can vary. Figures can be compiled using different criteria, or individuals may report the numbers in a way that favors their own agenda.

According to most of the people who take a professional interest in juvenile violence—people in government, law enforcement, social sciences, and education—the best source for crime statistics is the FBI's annual report, *Crime in the United States,* which is based on reports from over sixteen thousand law enforcement agencies covering 95 percent of the nation's population. Juvenile crime figures

are reported to the FBI by law enforcement agencies from around the nation. They are then compiled in the annual crime report along with breakdowns for gender, race, age group, and category of crime.

Interpreting these statistics is a major challenge even for the experts. Trying to come up with useful insights—for example, finding links between violent crimes and their causes—is an immense job. One problem is the validity of the numbers themselves. The FBI admits that its figures are not perfect, and that biases and misreporting and non-reporting creep into the statistics. Oddly enough, however, even the critics of the FBI statistics cannot agree about whether they err toward the low or the high side of how much juvenile violence actually occurs.

Some factors tend to make the numbers lower than they are in reality, and some factors tend to make them higher. For example, many acts of juvenile violence are never re-ported and many are never solved. Therefore it is possible that official statistics reflect only a fraction of all youth violence. On the other hand, law enforcement agencies admit that they frequently arrest multiple suspects for the same crime, and they frequently charge suspects with more severe crimes than they actually might have committed. Such practices tend to make the arrest statistics considerably higher.

For these kinds of reasons the numbers reported by the FBI may not be accurate. Nevertheless, even if they are high or low, the FBI statistics are generally accepted as approximately proportional to the true numbers. As such, they provide the best available information about trends and the growth or decline of youth violence.

No matter how inexact the FBI figures are, the year-to-year statistics show that juvenile violent crime is definitely increasing faster than the juvenile population is growing. In addition, juvenile violent crime is increasing faster than adult violent crime.

Murder

In 1989, the FBI reported that 11 percent of all murders (homicides) in the United States were committed by kids under the age of eighteen. In 1992 that figure had climbed to almost 15 percent. Two years later it was 17 percent.

Nationally, the number of juveniles who killed another person with a handgun quintupled between 1984 and 1994 (358 to 1,856, more than a 500 percent increase), according to a Northeastern University report submitted to the U.S. attorney general. And the Center to Prevent Handgun Violence reported that in 1995, 78 percent of all killings in which the victims were between thirteen and twenty were committed with guns.

Assault and robbery

The figures for juvenile violent crimes other than murder have also been climbing. From 1985 to 1994, the number of all violent crimes handled by juvenile courts doubled to fifty-four hundred cases. Compared with 1985, in 1994 juvenile courts handled 25 percent more rape cases, 53 percent more robbery cases, 134 percent more aggravated assault cases, and 91 percent more simple assault cases. During the same period, juvenile courts saw violations of gun laws increase 156 percent.

A simple assault is an attack, or a threatened attack, directed toward another person without using a deadly weapon. An aggravated assault is an attack or a threatened attack directed toward another person with the intention of hurting or killing that person with a deadly weapon. Robbery is an assault, simple or aggravated, with the intention of depriving another person of property or money.

Unlike other categories of violent crime, serious assaults by juveniles remained at a relatively constant rate from 1965 to the mid-1990s (between 9 and 12 percent of all reported cases). Juveniles were charged with committing 16 percent of all reported robberies in 1992.

Rape and dating violence

According to crime experts, most adult rapists begin their sexual violence during adolescence or even younger. FBI figures show that boys younger than eighteen account for 14 percent of all rape arrests in the United States. That

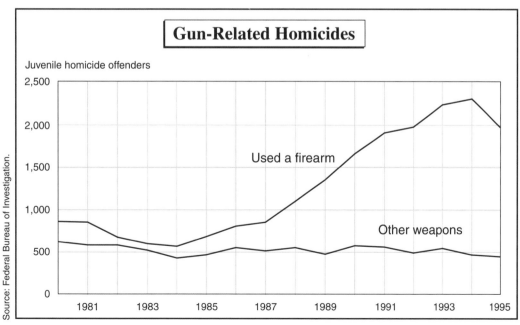

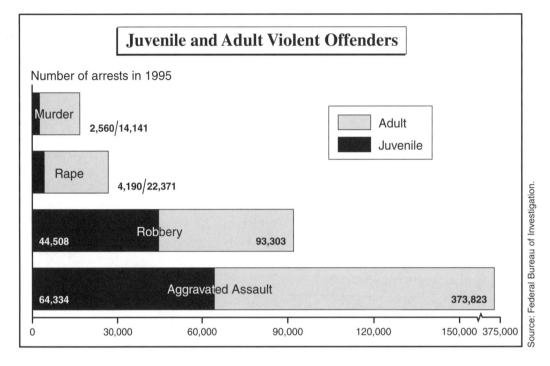

Juvenile and Adult Violent Offenders

Number of arrests in 1995

Murder 2,560/14,141

Rape 4,190/22,371

Robbery 44,508 93,303

Aggravated Assault 64,334 373,823

Adult
Juvenile

Source: Federal Bureau of Investigation.

translates to four thousand and in some instances five thousand juvenile arrests for rape each year. Over 5 percent of those boys are age fifteen and under.

Rape is often the ultimate result of what is known as dating violence. Dating violence ranges from verbal abuse to a slap in the face to harsher physical abuse including rape and even murder committed in a fit of jealous rage. The chief characteristic of dating violence is that there is sex and/or physical harm that is unwanted by one of the individuals. The overwhelming majority of perpetrators of dating violence are male, which explains why dating violence is sometimes called boyfriend violence.

According to a 1996 report from the Family Research Laboratory at the University of New Hampshire, up to 28 percent of teenagers in an intimate relationship are affected by dating violence. In another study conducted in 1992 at the University of Illinois, 36 percent of high school girls reported they had experienced some kind of violence on a date.

Dating violence is reported with nearly equal frequency in cities, towns, and suburban areas, according to the U.S.

Department of Justice, and it cuts across all racial and ethnic lines. But teens from families with incomes in the poverty range report the most cases, with the numbers decreasing with higher education and income levels.

In nearly all situations, however, dating violence is an aspect of teenage life that is usually hidden from parents and other adults. Of the high school girls who reported dating violence to the researchers in the Illinois study, only 4 percent had talked about it with a parent or other authority figure. A few had told peers, but almost all had remained silent.

Not all juvenile violence statistics are increasing

When the FBI released its crime figures in 1996 for the preceding year, a collective sigh of relief could be heard around the country. For the first time since 1983, violent crime had decreased. Among juveniles, the arrest rate for violent crimes had declined from 527.4 to 511.9 per 100,000 youth population age ten to seventeen. The juvenile homicide rate also dropped from 13.2 to 11.2 per 100,000 youth population age ten to seventeen.

Some analysts question whether juvenile violence is the primary factor behind the increases in violent crime rates. They point to the fact that even though juvenile arrests for violent crimes increased by 45 percent between 1982 and 1992, that is not much different than the 41 percent increase in adult arrests for violent crimes during the same period. If about 19 percent of the increase in violent crime is due to juveniles between the age of twelve and seventeen as the FBI states, then who is responsible for the other 81 percent? The FBI figures show that the arrests for thirty- to forty-nine-year-olds increased from 110,000 in 1980 to 270,000 in 1994, the largest increase of any age group in the last fifteen years. California's 1995 data show for the first time that thirty- to thirty-nine-year-olds were more likely to be arrested for a violent felony than ten- to nineteen-year-olds.

Though 19 percent of the increase in violent crime may be attributed to juveniles, apparently not all sectors of the juvenile population are equally responsible. One number relating to serious juvenile crimes that has not increased in the last two decades is the fraction of juveniles who commit the lion's share of teen violence. These kids who are repeatedly arrested for violent crimes are called serious and habitual offenders (SHO). Research by the Department of Justice has determined that SHO kids make up only 15 percent of all the teens arrested for violent crimes, yet they account for 75 to 82 percent of the offenses. The percentage of SHO juveniles has not noticeably increased since the 1960s.

Girls versus boys

Until the 1980s male juveniles accounted for more than 90 percent of juvenile violent crime arrests but starting about 1985 that began to change. By 1994 males were responsible for 77 percent of juvenile violent crimes and females were responsible for 23 percent.

Male and Female Violent Offenders

Arrests per 100,000 juveniles ages 10–17

Source: Office of Juvenile Justice and Delinquency Prevention.

Comparing the figures from 1994 with those from 1980, the increases in murder rates were different for young males than they were for females. Almost three times as many males under eighteen were arrested for murder in 1994 than in 1980 (about a 300 percent increase), while for females during the same period, the murder rates increased by about 16 percent. Some analysts attribute this difference in the growth of male and female teen violence to male gang violence, although the figures generally do not identify how much violence is due to gang activity.

The statistics generated in reports from the FBI and juvenile courts attempt to reconcile a variety of standards, inconsistencies, gaps, assumptions, estimates, and sometimes deceptions. Nowhere do statistics produce more disagreement and confusion than in the area of race. Many people are increasingly questioning the value of categorizing juvenile crimes in terms of the race of the offenders.

Race trends in teen violence

Officially, the Department of Justice recognizes only three loosely defined racial categories: black, other, and white. It defines black as a person having origins in any of the black racial groups of Africa. Other is defined as a person having origins in any of the indigenous peoples of North America, the Far East, Southeast Asia, the Indian subcontinent, or the Pacific Islands. It defines white as a person having origins in any of the indigenous peoples of Europe, North Africa, or the Middle East, a category that includes most Hispanics. With such broad, loose definitions, it is apparent why many people have asked why the government even bothers with racial categories at all.

In 1994, the Department of Justice's Office of Juvenile Justice and Delinquency Prevention (OJJDP) reported that: white teens were responsible for 57 percent of all cases of juvenile violence brought before juvenile courts, black teens were responsible for 40 percent, and teens of other races were responsible for 3 percent. Rates of increase for juvenile violent crimes between 1985 and 1994 were 94 percent for youth of other races, 78 percent for black youth, and 26 percent for white youth.

In recent years, juvenile violence has struck the African American communities particularly hard. Although African Americans of all ages make up only about 12 percent of the total population, 50 percent of all murder victims are African American. Enough of those victims are juveniles to make murder the leading cause of death among male African American teenagers. In 1990, 93 percent of African American murder victims were killed by other African Americans.

Though the figures indicate that gender and race somehow have a hand in shaping the statistics of juvenile violence, factors in the social and physical environment seem to play an even greater role.

Where does teen violence happen?

Teen violence is all too common right where young people live, particularly in the nation's troubled urban areas. Some geographical areas of the country have a higher incidence of teen violence than others. The only thing that these regions have in common is that they all include large urban areas. In many cities some neighborhoods seem like war zones, and the teens who live there are both the soldiers and the victims. Still, some cities have much higher rates of juvenile violence than others.

The 1995 FBI report on national arrest figures showed five urban areas with juvenile violent crime arrest rates over 1,000 per 100,000 juveniles: Hudson County (Jersey City), New Jersey (1,302); New York City, New York (1,247); San Francisco, California (1,080); Racine, Wisconsin (1,059); and Fulton County (Atlanta), Georgia (1,056).

Although these areas have prominent juvenile crime rates that exceed 1 percent of their juvenile populations, violent crime is increasing in all parts of the country. Between 1984 and 1994, the average of violent crime arrests per 100,000 juveniles in all rural areas went from 46 to 135, in all suburban areas from 102 to 236, and in all urban areas from 150 to 540.

Violence at school

City school grounds are a frequent site of teen violence. As an indicator of how big the problem is, the security personnel for New York City schools make up the ninth-largest police force in the nation, reported Martin Haberman and Vicky Dill in the Summer 1995 issue of *Educational Forum.*

In a 1995 study reported in *USA Today,* Arlene Stiffman, a professor at the George Warren Brown School of Social Work, found one-third of inner-city students said they had seen at least one physical attack or robbery involving teens on campus during the preceding year, and 25 percent said that teachers at their school had been injured by students. Furthermore, the study indicated that the neighborhoods near inner-city schools tended to be more dangerous than other nearby similar areas that were not near schools.

In an attempt to curb teen violence at school, this Brooklyn, New York, high school requires students to pass through a metal detector each morning.

A 1995 report by the American Federation of Teachers found that during the previous year more than 3 million students nationwide reported being assaulted or threatened with assault at school, and that the daily average number of children who did not attend school because they were afraid of being attacked was approximately 160,000. Teachers across the country also reported that they were forced to spend much of their time in class defusing potentially violent problems, which left less time for teaching and learning.

Violence at home

The other place where teen violence is especially likely to occur is inside the home. Statistics confirm that violence—spouse abuse, child abuse, beatings—inside the home is widespread. A 1996 study by the National Center on Child Abuse and Neglect (a department of the U.S. Department of Health and Human Services) revealed that in over half of the families in which the adult woman is physically abused by the adult man, the children are also physically assaulted. The study also concluded that children from violent homes are almost twice as likely to engage in violence as children from homes where there is no physical abuse.

In 1995 over 3 million children were reported abused or neglected in the United States, according to a state-by-state survey conducted by the National Committee to Prevent Child Abuse. That represented a rise of 2 percent over the 1994 figure. Furthermore, a 1996 report by the U.S. Department of Health and Human Services found that the number of child abuse and neglect cases nearly doubled between 1986 and 1993 to 2.8 million cases, and that is just the cases that were reported. A 1995 Gallup poll of parents found that physical abuse may be as much as six times higher than the official reported number and sexual abuse may be ten times higher. Events within a family that leave a person injured physically or mentally or that result in death are not just a "family matter" in the eyes of the courts. Family violence is a crime.

Violent America

Figures from the World Health Organization's National Center for Health Statistics show the level of youth violence varies greatly from country to country. The WHO's 1994 homicide rates (murders per 100,000 people) for males age fifteen to twenty-four, listed highest to lowest, were: United States, 21.9; Scotland, 5.0; New Zealand, 4.0; Israel, 3.7; Canada, 2.9; France, 1.4; Greece, 1.4; Ireland, 1.2; Poland, 1.2; Great Britain, 1.2; Japan, 0.5.

Clearly the United States leads the industrialized world in violent youth crime, but it is also in a league by itself in the number of deaths caused by shooting. According to the Center to Prevent Handgun Violence, in 1990 the number of deaths caused by handguns (including homicides and accidents) in some representative countries were: United States, 10,567; Switzerland, 91; Japan, 87; Great Britain, 22; Australia, 10.

Furthermore, according to the United Nations Interregional Crime and Justice Research Institute, the United States has the highest statistics in other areas that affect teen violence, including child poverty, crime, and imprisonment. Compared with Europe, for example, the United States has more than twice as much child poverty and crime per 100,000 people, and more than five times as many of its citizens are imprisoned.

Public opinion translated into law

Juvenile crime is certainly growing, and the worst cases involve brutality made all the more shocking by the age of the offenders. The statistics, however, clearly show that overall, juvenile violent crime is growing at essentially the same rate as adult violent crime and, as the National Council on Crime and Delinquency has stated in several subsequent annual reports, an individual is much more likely to be victimized by an adult than by a juvenile. Yet, the public and most of the nation's political leaders seem to believe that the greatest contribution to violent crime comes from juveniles. The root of this belief may be that the sight of young people committing violent crimes is so frightening,

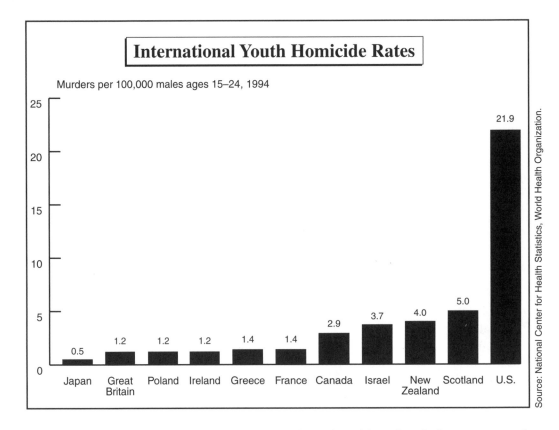

International Youth Homicide Rates

Murders per 100,000 males ages 15–24, 1994

Source: National Center for Health Statistics, World Health Organization.

Japan	Great Britain	Poland	Ireland	Greece	France	Canada	Israel	New Zealand	Scotland	U.S.
0.5	1.2	1.2	1.2	1.4	1.4	2.9	3.7	4.0	5.0	21.9

so repellant, and so heartbreaking that it leaves a much deeper impression than dry statistics. Furthermore, violent juvenile crime often provides sensational material for the television and print media, making a grossly overblown picture of juvenile crime inevitable. A 1995 report from the Coalition for Juvenile Justice stated that much of the drive toward treating juveniles as adults "is a political reaction to public opinion fueled by disproportionate media coverage of youth crime."

Public opinion has a great deal of power to influence the laws and government policy, but the public's view of teen violence is sometimes limited or distorted by the media, the police, and political leaders. The media tend to concentrate on the most sensational incidents even though they are uncommon. Sometimes the police also contribute to misconceptions by inadvertently creating higher arrest figures for types of crimes where the perpetrators are easier to identify and catch (gang violence, for example). Many politically motivated leaders favor actions that produce immediate results—like more arrests—with more regard for the next election than long-term reduction of the conditions that breed teen violence.

Less than one-half of 1 percent of the kids

Although the number of juveniles arrested for violent crimes has certainly increased, and although juveniles have been responsible for more than their share of violent crime for generations, the data clearly reveal that juveniles are *not* responsible for most of the increases in violent crimes. The FBI figures are very clear on this point: adults were responsible for 74 percent of the overall increase in violent crimes from 1985 to 1994.

There is no question that the problem of juvenile crime is very serious and the country badly needs better, more effective means of reducing and preventing teen violence. Nevertheless, of all the juveniles living in the United States in 1994, fewer than one-half of 1 percent were arrested for a violent offense—less than one in two hundred. Furthermore, most of the worst teen violence was committed by only a small portion of those kids.

2

The Causes
of Teen Violence

MOST OF THE experts who have studied teen violence agree that the violent acts committed by teenagers—assaults, shootings, armed robberies, rapes—cannot all be explained by a single reason. Reporting that a violent young person is bad, irresponsible, lazy, or immoral gives little insight to the variety of reasons and influences behind the behavior. To begin to understand what is most likely to make a teenager capable of brutality and what conditions are most likely to trigger juvenile violence, it is necessary to look deeper into the lives of violent teens, the society that surrounds them, and the statistics of their crimes.

The "nature versus nurture" controversy

Even with all the statistics and studies of teen violence, experts disagree on some of the fundamental notions about the causes of teen violence. One of the longest lasting disagreements surrounds what is called the "nature versus nurture" controversy. In this sense, "nature" refers to the idea that some people are naturally violent as a result of irresistible biological compulsions. In other words, according to the nature theory it is biology—primarily the genes a person has inherited—that makes some teens behave violently. "Nurture," on the other hand, refers to the ways people *learn* to behave violently as a result of their upbringing and surroundings. Experiencing or witnessing parental violence, living in a violent neighborhood, watching violent movies—

these and many other environmental influences have been suggested as factors that nurture violence in teens.

Is there such a creature as a born criminal? A century ago, a popular theory existed that proposed some people were not only born with criminal traits, but also that these people could actually be identified by physical characteristics like sloping foreheads and massive jaws. Over time science has found very little proof that criminals can be recognized by their appearance, and this theory has fallen by the wayside. There remains, however, a persistent thread of evidence supporting the existence of a genetic factor that causes a tendency toward criminal behavior.

A great deal of research has focused on finding a relationship between criminal behavior and hereditary traits.

'Forgive my father, for I have sinned.'

Some of the inherited factors that have been studied are the extra Y chromosome that occasionally appears in males, various congenital (inherited) learning disabilities, and certain enzyme deficiencies. So far, however, behavioral scientists have found no conclusive results from all the attempts to tie juvenile violence and other criminal behavior to biology, genetics, and biochemistry. The most that can be said is that people's tendencies to be violent vary greatly and that these tendencies may be affected by biological causes. In other words, research supports the possibility that biological causes influence juvenile violence.

In the last twenty years, research has amassed a mountain of evidence in support of the fact that most violent criminals share a background that includes abusive childhoods, certain forms of brain damage, and mental illness. While one or two of these conditions do not specifically cause violent behavior, it appears increasingly likely that all three factors together are able to turn some people into violent criminals. If this is the case, it would mean that violent behavior may be largely independent of genetics and race.

The real-life importance to the "nature versus nurture" argument that should not be ignored is that, if genetic or other biological factors form the reason behind a juvenile's violent acts, the legal system would deal with that person's crimes quite differently than if the youngster had learned to be violent from an abusive family setting, or was violent as the result of a brain injury that could be treated. Nature versus nurture would spell the difference between judging a person to be an irredeemable criminal and attempting to change the person's behavior through education, counseling, and medical treatment.

The immediate cause versus the underlying cause

When discussing the causes of juvenile violence, it is useful to distinguish between the underlying cause and the immediate cause (sometimes called the ultimate cause and the proximate cause) of violent behavior.

Many youths eventually learn that they must pay for their crimes like their adult counter-parts. Here, a member of the Crazy Riders gang serves time in a Los Angeles youth prison.

When the police asked a young suspect in a recent shoot-ing in Los Angeles why he had shot a member of a rival gang, the boy answered, "That dude was mad-dogging me so I lit him up." According to the boy, the immediate cause for the shooting was the aggressive look (mad-dogging) he was getting from the victim. The underlying cause was probably more complex, perhaps related to a desire to earn respect and stature among his gang members.

Frequently the immediate cause for a violent crime seems meaningless, thus the term "senseless violence." People who seek to understand and halt juvenile violence try to look beyond the immediate causes for the long-term, underlying causes that lead a young person to cross the line into violence. Some examples of the underlying causes that might lead to violent behavior in some individ-uals are anger and a lack of empathy resulting from child-hood abuse, an inherited tendency to be violent, a need for respect and attention where there is none at home, and even brain damage.

Although there may be genetic factors contributing to the underlying causes of teen violence, social workers and police cannot change these influences. Instead au-thorities and social services tend to focus on environmen-tal and social factors that potentially can be controlled.

These factors—the influences of nurture—include violence or neglect in the home, drugs, the availability of handguns, and inner-city conditions.

Unhappy families

In the 1980s, the National Council on Child Abuse and Family Violence found that a disproportionately large number of juveniles who commit violent crimes come from unhappy families. An unhappy family is defined as a family with marital problems, substance abuse, unaffectionate parents, lack of family communications, high stress and tension, or physical violence.

Although unhappy families are by no means restricted to single-parent homes, a disproportionately large number of troubled teens come from single-parent homes. For example, of seventy adolescent murderers reported in a 1972 study in the *Journal of Criminal Justice,* three-quarters of these juveniles came from single-parent homes.

More recent research also reinforces the idea that the roots of violence begin before preschool. A 1993 study by the Harvard School of Public Health, examining the early childhood years of violent teenagers, confirmed that they shared certain experiences related to the quality of their early relationships with their parents. These included parental criminal behavior, parental drug use, physical and emotional abuse by parents, the lack of parental involvement and supervision, and the absence of one parent due to divorce or separation.

Along the same lines, the Office of Juvenile Justice and Delinquency Prevention (OJJDP) conducted a study that found being seriously neglected as a child is almost as likely to produce juvenile violence as growing up in a violent family.

A major problem for many communities is the lack of supervision provided for their young people. Inadequate parental supervision can be the result of many factors. With single parents working long hours or both parents working, there is a greater chance that the children will lack adult supervision and role models. Overly liberal parents may feel they do not want to interfere by supervising their children's developing personal lives. Overly strict parents can drive a child from the home. For these and other reasons, all across the nation large numbers of young people are left on their own to figure out how to meet most of their emotional and psychological needs, especially during the hours after school.

Growing up in a violent home

Charles R. is a bright and talkative fifteen-year-old from San Diego. When a classmate threw dirt on Charles's jeans, Charles, then thirteen, beat him up. The boy he attacked ended up with, among other injuries, a broken arm. Charles was charged with juvenile assault for the second time in his young life and placed on probation.

"I know I have a temper. When I get mad, I am going to hit someone, anyone, whoever is in my way," Charles said in a 1996 interview in the *San Diego Union-Tribune*.

Charles knows exactly where he got the idea for hitting people. "I learned from my father that punching and slapping are what you do when someone makes you angry."

The single greatest predictor of violence

When it comes to learning violence at home, Charles is not alone. A major 1994 report by the American Psychological Association (APA) stated unequivocally that the roots of violence are in the home. The single greatest predictor of violence during the teen years is a personal history of violence in the home, according to the APA's Commission on Youth and Violence. Furthermore, parents who themselves have a history of violence raise children with a greater than normal chance of becoming violent.

The APA believes that violence is not a natural state but rather is learned by watching parents and peers. Social influences, life on the streets, interactions at school, images of violence in the mass media—all these can help inflame violent behavior, but, according to the APA, the family setting is the primary influence.

The APA is not the only group of experts who believe that the best predictor of violent behavior during a person's teenage years is exposure to violence at home. According to a 1992 U.S. Department of Justice report, 68 percent of all youths arrested for violent crimes had a prior history of childhood abuse and neglect. A great many sociologists, criminologists, judges, and probation officers agree that the primary cause of violence among juveniles is being raised in a violent family.

Research repeatedly shows that growing numbers of children and adolescents are victims of physical and sexual violence at home. According to a 1996 report by the U.S. Department of Health and Human Services, child abuse by parents and stepparents as well as other forms of family violence are at record levels in the United States. That report found that the number of child abuse and neglect cases (reported and unreported) rose from an estimated 1.4 million in 1986 to an estimated 2.8 million in 1993 to 3.1 million in 1995.

The National Committee to Prevent Child Abuse (NCPCA) calculates, based on reports from child protective services in all fifty states, that 4 percent of all American children suffer from extensive abuse or neglect. That is over 3 million children in 1995, and the director of the NCPCA says that these figures are low. The FBI agrees that most forms of domestic violence other than murder are grossly underreported.

Terence Thornberry, a professor at the School of Criminal Justice at the State University of New York at Albany studied one thousand students attending public schools in Rochester, New York, from grades seven to twelve. His project interviewed the students every six months and collected relevant data from police, schools, and social services agencies. The results of this study, published at the end of 1994, found that when a child's history combined abuse and maltreatment in a family where the parents also fought with each other, the chances of that child becoming violent increased to twice the rate of youth violence in adolescents from nonviolent families. This scientifically controlled, six-year study found that this rate applied equally to boys and girls, all races, and all social classes.

Unanswered questions about violent homes

Despite all the research, crime experts and psychologists report they do not really understand all of the long-term effects of growing up in a violent home. Though many questions remain, research clearly supports the notion that a violent home pushes a child toward juvenile violence. Besides learning how to physically harm others, children who live with domestic violence may come to believe that violence is the normal response to problems in personal relationships. Even when it is not directed toward the children, domestic violence makes effective parenting impossible.

None of this is to say that domestic violence or neglect *have to* result in a young person becoming violent. Vast numbers of teens are raised in adverse family situations without becoming violent criminals. Likewise, many juveniles from apparently well-balanced families do become violent. One of the most pressing questions in current research is what makes one child violent when another in the same conditions, even a brother or sister, does not become violent. The latest figures suggest that the most likely factors include how early the violence or neglect began, how frequent and severe it was, and if other adults or older children were present who could prevent or reduce violence and neglect. So far though, the experts have drawn only one meaningful conclusion from the statistics

A young boy sits on his mother's lap inside a shelter for abused women and children. Children from abusive homes are more likely to commit crimes as teenagers than children reared in nonabusive environments.

linking troubled families to higher incidences of teen violence: It appears certain that children from unhappy families have a greater chance of becoming violent than children raised in happier settings.

Drug use

There is another quite different link between the home and teen violence: drugs. The rate of drug abuse by thirty- to forty-year-olds, as measured by hospital emergency room statistics, has increased twelvefold since 1980. The NCPCA estimates that 9 to 10 million children under the age of eighteen are directly affected by substance-abusing parents. Two-thirds of abuse and neglect cases, according to family court statistics, are related to parents' drug abuse. The well-documented link between child abuse and the later appearance of violent behavior in abused children is often related, therefore, to parental drug use.

Drug use by teens is also being examined as a possible contributing factor to juvenile violence. Some behavior-altering substances, specifically alcohol, crack and other forms of cocaine, and amphetamines, have been closely linked with violence. Whether or not there is a cause and effect, however, is not clear. Some say violent juveniles are more likely to use drugs, while others assert that drug-using juveniles are more likely to be violent. In other words, they disagree about whether violent behavior or drug use comes first.

American youth tend to exhibit the characteristics of society at large, and American society is a drug-consuming society. In the last two decades, drug use by American youth has lessened and then escalated again. After several years of decreasing drug use by teenagers, a survey conducted by the University of Michigan in 1991 found drug use, except for alcohol, to be the lowest since the early 1980s. The study showed that almost 60 percent of high school seniors had used alcohol in the month prior to the survey while less than 20 percent had used some illicit drug. By the mid-1990s, drug use by teens was rising again.

Although the correlation between drug use and teen violence is not clear, teens who commit violent crimes are generally more involved in drug use than their peers.

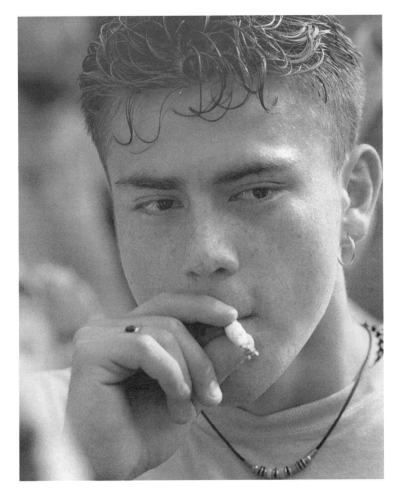

FBI statistics show nationwide juvenile arrests for marijuana going from less than twenty thousand in 1991 to over sixty thousand in 1995. Furthermore, according to 1995 figures, just over 50 percent of teens arrested for juvenile delinquency of all types had used marijuana recently—up from 18 percent in 1990. While marijuana is not generally considered to lead to violent behavior, rising arrest rates for marijuana possession are assumed by police to indicate a resurgence of interest in drug use among youth.

Drugs and aggression

On the other hand, cocaine (coke, crack, rock), amphetamines (speed, crystal, meth, crank, ecstasy, ice), and alcohol are often described as potential on-ramps to the road of violent behavior. According to criminologists, drugs and alcohol do not make most people behave violently, but they can make a violent outcome more likely. Judgment is clouded by being high or drunk and inhibitions are lost. Maybe a drug deal goes bad, or maybe a group of kids are high, jittery and wired, feeling brave, feeling like they have to do something—the stage is set for violence.

According to an extensive review of research literature published in the journal *Alcohol Health and Research* in 1993, alcohol abuse in youths between the age of twelve and twenty-four causes increased aggression in males both during those ages and later in life. In this study as in others, it may be impossible to determine if there is a direct link between violent crime and the use of alcohol (and other drugs), because a large percentage of teens arrested for violent crimes use alcohol and other drugs so routinely that virtually all of their activities involve prior or current use. The research suggests that teens who commit violent crimes are in general more involved in delinquency, alcohol, and drug use than their peers. This research review found that there was a trend for adolescents to be more likely to use alcohol immediately before a violent crime than before a crime motivated by profit.

Still, the relationship between drug use and violence is not a proven fact. A drunk or high teenager does not automatically become violent. Nor are a majority of violent teen crimes committed while under the influence. All that can be said with certainty is that drug abuse and violence are intertwined for some violent youth; for others, drug use is not a factor in their violent acts.

The proliferation of handguns

One major contributor to the escalation of teen violence that experts do generally agree upon is the easy availability of guns. According to a 1996 report by the American Academy of Child and Adolescent Psychiatry, every day in the United States ten children under the age of nineteen are killed with handguns in homicides, suicides, or accidents.

Many more are injured by guns. In fact, according to the Center to Prevent Handgun Violence, fourteen out of fifteen juvenile murders were shootings in 1992.

Guns figure in more than 75 percent of adolescent homicides and more than half of teenage suicides. An astounding number of children either own a gun or know how to get one. A national survey by the Centers for Disease Control and Prevention in Atlanta found that 4 percent of the country's high school students had carried a gun at least once in the month prior to the survey. In some schools the figure was considerably higher. Up to one-third of the students who said they had taken a gun to school reported that they had actually fired their guns at another person at least once.

By all indications, guns are easier than ever to obtain. In Chicago, San Diego, and New York, just to name three examples of cities with laws designed to make it difficult to acquire a gun quickly, police on gang details say that a kid can get a cheap pistol within two hours for as little as twenty dollars. And every city has teens who are well versed in gun availability. In a 1996 article in the *San Diego Union-Tribune,* a member of the San Diego Police Department's gang unit described a tenth grader who could name every popular gun model ranging from an easily concealed Raven semiautomatic to an Intratec mini–machine gun. The teen added, "As long as you got the money, you can get a gun."

Gun violence soars

With so many guns currently in the hands of young people, routine fights often turn into gun battles. Fearing for their safety, more and more teens are taking up arms in a brutal cycle of escalating violence. In 1992, according to the Centers for Disease Control and Prevention, the nationwide number of juvenile murders not involving guns grew 20 percent while the number that did involve guns grew 300 percent.

Quoted in a 1996 U.S. Department of Justice Fact Sheet, a probation officer in Los Angeles, who supervises many juvenile gang members, estimated that 80 percent had been

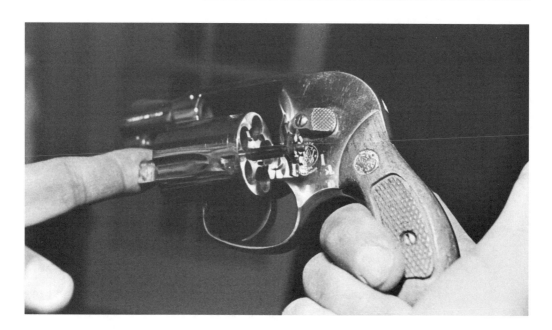

wounded by gunfire at least once in their lives and over 20 percent have been shot more than once. "The type of firepower and the access to guns have both increased radically even as the age of the shooters has dropped," stated the probation officer.

Easy access to handguns has contributed to the problem of teen violence. Seventy-five percent of adolescent homicides and 50 percent of teen suicides are gun-related.

A political response to teen gun violence

A growing number of the nation's political leaders, convinced that the easy availability of handguns is the driving force behind the growth in teen violence, are looking for ways to reverse this dangerous trend. On October 10, 1996, eighty-four senators from both political parties joined President Bill Clinton in not only urging all young Americans to voluntarily sign a pledge designed to decrease gun violence, but also they asked the youth of America to make the following vow:

> I pledge I will never bring a gun to school; that I will never use a gun to settle a dispute; and that I will use my influence with my friends to keep them from using guns to settle disputes.

The principal author of this pledge, Senator Bill Bradley, summed up the feeling among many Americans when he said in a speech to Congress:

An epidemic of violence is ensnaring our children at an alarming rate. It is time to make it unfashionable to carry a gun to school. It is time to make it unacceptable to resolve a dispute with a gun. It is time to give young people in this country a chance to stand up and retake their schools and their neighborhoods.

Teen sexual violence

Just like some communities have higher rates of juvenile shootings, some communities have higher rates of teen sexual violence. Dr. Jane Hood, a sociologist at the University of New Mexico, has studied this phenomenon in cities around the United States. She found that communities where a large percentage of families have weak or nonexistent father-son relationships, where other forms of violence among young males are common, and where there is a communitywide acceptance of male toughness tended to have a much greater incidence of teen rape than communities without these characteristics.

Sexual violence in teens has one major thing in common with sexual violence in adults: anger. Sociologists and psychologists agree that rape, no matter what the age of the rapist, has little to do with sex and everything to do with rage.

Inner-city violence

While the debate about the causes of teen violence often focuses on the make-believe violence on television and in movies, the greater behavioral influence may be the real-life violence that many inner-city teens live through every day of their lives. Gang violence and the ability of ordinary teens to easily obtain guns make murder an almost commonplace event in the cores of America's cities.

According to a 1995 Washington University study of high school–age youngsters in St. Louis, teens who are growing up in what amounts to a war zone are likely to end up behaving like they are in a war. Fully half of the 797 kids in the study had witnessed a killing or serious beating, 39 percent had a friend who was beaten or killed, and 50 percent had been in a serious physical fight themselves. The report concluded that the more violence teens were exposed to on the streets and in school, the more likely they were to be violent themselves, to abuse drugs and alcohol, and to lose hope for the future.

Violence is certainly no stranger to inner-city teens. The tensions that lead to this violence are rooted in the problems of urban communities. Anger, despair, and frustration are symptoms of the joblessness, boredom, and lack of opportunity that characterize the lives of the urban poor.

Poverty

In a 1994 report to American educators, U.S. surgeon general Joycelyn Elders stated in a speech to law enforcement leaders:

> The violence in our society is not the result of any racial or ethnic risk factor, but rather, it reflects an association between violence and poverty. Because of its deep roots in poverty, violence has a disproportionately greater effect on racial and ethnic minorities since 50 percent of African American children are poor, 33 percent of Hispanic children are poor, and up to 90 percent of all Native American children live in poverty.

Poverty has been repeatedly shown to be a major factor in breeding child abuse and violent youngsters. Poor communities frequently have higher than average rates of juvenile crime. According to OJJDP statistics, more than 35 million Americans are officially poor, and about 10 million of those are under the age of sixteen. In 1996 one out of every five American children lived in poverty, and half of those lived in destitution (family income less than $6,000 per year). Furthermore, poverty is increasing in the United States. In 1975, 6 percent of young children who lived in families with one full-time worker were poor. By 1994 that figure had gone up to 15 percent. In the last twenty-five years, poverty among the young has risen 25 percent.

Poor people are increasingly hemmed into poor neighborhoods with high crime and violence, substandard schools, and a lack of opportunity and accessible jobs. The number of people living in neighborhoods of concentrated poverty (where more than 40 percent of the households are officially poor) went up by 75 percent from 1970 to 1980, and then doubled between 1980 and 1990.

Drinking and violence are common in this young girl's poor Virginia neighborhood. Poverty is a primary predictor of teenage crime.

Some observers have suggested that poor communities encourage their youngsters to be violent. According to the OJJDP, however, most recent studies indicate that teen violence in poor neighborhoods is more closely related to histories of neglect and emotional abuse of children than to community acceptance of violence.

No simple explanation

Clearly there is no simple or single explanation that accounts for the way violence by and against teens has grown. Research, surveys, and personal beliefs attempt to pin the blame on many things: the easy availability of guns, the effects of drugs and alcohol, the battle for control of drug trafficking, gang culture, poverty, single-parent homes and the breakdown of the family, parenting that is too liberal, parenting that is too strict, poor education, poor housing, and unemployment. It has even been suggested that food additives cause violent behavior in juveniles. Perhaps all of these influences and others still unrecognized can contribute to teenage violence at different times. At this time, however, not even the experts can predict with absolute confidence what combination of circumstances will definitely produce violent behavior in a young person.

All of these potentially contributing factors are real-life conditions facing teens today. Many people, however, feel that the make-believe worlds presented to teens through television, movies, and music influence them toward violence as much as any other experience, and maybe more.

3

The Media and Teen Violence

VIOLENCE IN THE MEDIA reaches a wide and varied audience, and the ways it influences people may be different than the way exposure to real-life violence influences people. Many people believe the violence portrayed by the media—television, movies, popular music, and even the news—is a primary reason for the increase in teen violence in the United States. Violence makes a daily appearance in almost every home in the country: murder and mayhem is almost mandatory in some of the commercial and cable programming, brutality and killing arrives via cable and video, and violent lyrics burst from some of the most popular music.

Violent images: movies and television

The American Psychological Association named three factors found in homes that contribute the most to a child's becoming violent: child abuse and neglect, family violence such as spouse abuse, and the violence depicted in movies and television programming. The commission's report concluded:

> Prolonged exposure to violent images produces an impact that reaches as deep and lasts as long as other contributors to violence, increasing the fear of becoming a victim, desensitizing the viewer to violence, and increasing the viewer's appetite for engaging in violence.

44

Two U.S. surgeons general have publicly supported the position that excessive exposure to media violence can trigger aggressive behavior. The American Medical Association, the American Pediatric Association, the American Academy of Child Psychiatry, and the American Psychological Association have taken similar positions.

The psychologists, psychiatrists, and physicians of these associations are not the only people to speak out against the amount of screen violence available to youth. Reactions against the rising tide of violence on television and in the movies have come from all walks of society and the entire political spectrum. Democratic and Republican presidential candidates, surgeons general, police organizations, parent groups, and the American Psychological Association are just a few of the individuals and groups who have publicly deplored the level of violence in popular entertainment.

How violence is depicted on the screen

On the screen, violence is frequently portrayed as a quick, exciting way to settle an argument or get rid of an opponent. Parent groups and some government leaders are voicing concern that today's screens are teaching kids to treat violence like an ordinary fact of life. They wonder if in the neighborhoods where violence actually is an ordinary fact of life, television and movies helped make it that way.

A five-year study by the American Psychological Association found that the average child witnesses 8,000 murders and 100,000 other acts of violence on television by the seventh grade. They could add 264 more killings to that number if they watched the movie *Die Hard 2,* a fairly typical, extremely popular action film. Many of the most successful movies in terms of box office receipts are full of graphic violence. *Scream,* just one of a series of bloodbath movies from director Wes Craven, was one of the biggest money-making films in any category in 1996–97. It graphically shows the slashing murders of several teenagers by a pair of homicidal maniacs who are themselves popular seniors at the local high school. Almost any gangster or police film will raise the number of murders seen through a young viewer's eyes by double digits. Even the Oscar winner *Braveheart* is filled with gory ways that medieval warriors put their enemies to death.

Parents who want to keep their young children away from movies like these can probably do so. Then the youngsters turn on the television, often with minimal supervision or guidance, and are deluged with violence in the news or on prime-time action dramas.

The National Center for Media and Values found that prime-time commercial television programs average about fifty crimes, including a dozen murders, every hour. At that rate, they say, the television murder rate is roughly a thousand times higher than in the real world. According to the center, even Saturday morning cartoons are not free of violence, averaging twenty-five violent acts per hour.

The influence of screen violence on teens

According to the American Psychological Association study, repeated exposure to violence makes violence seem more normal and acceptable. Furthermore, the study showed that the results are essentially the same whether this exposure is to real-life violence or two-dimensional violence on a screen. In other words, a child who watches realistic violence on a television screen is affected to the same extent as a child who witnesses fights at school and gang shootings in the neighborhood.

While it remains unproven that violent entertainment causes violent behavior, a 1996 study commissioned by the cable television industry makes a strong connection between what people see and how they feel. The National Television Violence Study concluded that the side effects of viewing television violence include learning to behave violently, becoming more desensitized to the consequences of violence, and becoming more fearful of being attacked. The study also found that people who watch a lot of television generally overestimate the amount of violence in their cities.

The American Academy of Child and Adolescent Psychiatry (AACAP), noting that the average American child watches three to four hours of television daily, contends that the contents of TV programming are a powerful influence on the values and behaviors of children. This organization of psychiatrists points out that there have been hundreds of studies over the years on the ways viewing violence on television affects children and teenagers. According to the AACAP, most of the evidence shows that children become immune to the horror of violence, come to accept violence as a way to solve problems, imitate the violence they see, and often start picturing themselves as similar to a particular victimizer. The AACAP asserts that the impact of viewing television violence may show up immediately, or it may appear years later as an increased tendency toward violence.

Some influential people in the government agree with the AACAP. In 1994, Surgeon General Joycelyn Elders said:

> By portraying violence as the normal means of conflict resolution, the media gives youth the message that violence is

When children are exposed to repeated acts of violence on television, they may learn that violence is acceptable in society. Some children imitate television violence in an effort to solve their problems.

socially acceptable and the best way to solve problems. After more than 10 years of research, we know that a correlation exists between violence on television and aggressive behavior by children.

While the correlation referred to by Elders does not amount to proof that violence on television causes consistent and predictable increases in aggressive behavior in children, a great deal of research does support it. Of the many researchers who have studied the relationship between television violence and real-world violence, Leonard D. Eron and his colleagues have conducted the longest-running investigation. They studied hundreds of young males at ten-year intervals over a period of thirty years. What they found was that the leading predictor of how violent a nineteen-year-old would be was the level of violence on television that he preferred when he was eight. Dr. Eron was not saying that years of viewing violent television necessarily make a nineteen-year-old violent, but that television violence is a key factor in helping already existing violent tendencies to develop. According to Eron's research, viewing violence on television as a young child may help people who already have violent tendencies decide to adopt violent methods for solving problems.

Former U.S. surgeon general Joycelyn Elders expressed concern about aggression in children and its relation to television violence.

Other studies that support Elder's claim to a correlation between viewing violence and real-life youth violence are based on increases in violence following the introduction of television to an area. Two years after television was introduced to remote Notel, Canada, physical aggression among children increased 160 percent. Another study looked at the effects of childhood exposure to television on roughly comparable white populations of the United States, Canada, and South Africa. Fifteen years after television was introduced to the United States and Canada, white homicide deaths had risen over 90 percent.

When television arrived in South Africa, the homicide rate among whites, which had been dropping, started climbing and within twelve years had increased by 130 percent.

Society's reaction to screen violence

With high body counts showing up regularly in visual entertainment as diverse as action movies and Saturday morning cartoons, it is tempting to place at least part of the blame for growing teen violence on movies and television. People who would like to see less violence on America's screens suggest that the rise in urban violence parallels the rise in violent content in movies and television programs, although conflicting statistics are presented by opponents and defenders of television programming. Despite all the research and criticism, the case for the harmful influence of screen violence is not absolutely airtight. Though many people strongly suspect that there is a definite link between violence in the media and violence in the streets and they defend their position as intuitive and obvious, such a direct link still has not been scientifically proven.

In 1996 the Center for Communication at the University of California at Los Angeles joined with the magazine *U.S. News & World Report* to discover what Americans really think of the content of commercial television. They decided to compare the opinions of viewers with the opinions of people responsible for program content, so they conducted a survey of 1,000 randomly selected adult viewers and 570 people who were influential in television and movies.

This was not a scientific survey, but it is useful as an indicator of how Americans feel about television programming. The results showed that two-thirds of the public believed television does contribute to violence and other social problems like divorce and teen pregnancy. Surprisingly, fully half of the television industry people agreed that TV has a negative impact on the country. Furthermore, a majority of the industry people said their industry was doing only a fair to poor job in encouraging lawful behavior and respect for police. Over 90 percent of viewers believed that television contributes directly to violence in the country and almost 80 percent of industry people shared that view.

On the other hand, the fact that portrayed violence and real violence have both been increasing could just be a coincidence. Half of those entertainment industry people in the survey believe that the entertainment industry is having a negative impact on the country in terms of violence and other social issues, but the other half feels differently. Those media insiders and some behavioral scientists continue to assert that viewing violence does not lead to violent behavior. After all, goes one of the standard defenses of screen violence, other countries show the same movies and their societies are not nearly as violent as the United States. Todd Gitlin, a professor of sociology at the Univer-

sity of California, Berkeley, has stated: "Images don't spill blood. Rage, equipped with guns, does. Desperation does. Revenge does. . . . The drug trade does; poverty does; unemployment does."

Resistance to curtailing screen violence

If so many people in the television industry feel that programming contributes to violence, why do they continue to show so much? The answers they gave centered on their perception that violence sells advertising, which means violence is what people want to see. Since they are only providing what the public has demonstrated that it wants, they believe, the industry is not to blame.

Attempts to regulate the amount of violence portrayed on television and in the movies are likely to fail for several reasons, but the primary reason is the First Amendment to the Constitution guaranteeing freedom of speech. The same freedom that allows people to voice their opposition to violent movies also allows those movies to continue playing. Prohibiting what some people find offensive runs against the whole idea of free speech.

Furthermore, one function of popular visual entertainment has always been to serve as a mirror of society, so as long as society is riddled with violence, violence will show up on screens. In fact, some opponents of the crusade against media violence believe that the politicians and other leaders are focusing on movie and television violence because they are helpless to overcome the real causes of violence in America. In other words, media violence is an easy target but not the real one.

How violence is depicted in music

Violence in the media is certainly not limited to visual depictions. There are plenty of violent auditory images as well. The lyrics to some extremely popular songs shock many adults, although that in itself is nothing new. Popular music has long included violent references, but recent concerns focus on the ways violence, including attacking police and women, is encouraged and glamorized in some

A casualty of violence himself, Notorious B.I.G.'s rap lyrics include violent images of gang warfare and retaliation.

music. Some bands and their promoters are getting rich singing about the violent world of gang life, the degradation of women, suicide as a solution to a teenager's problems, and the use of drugs and alcohol.

In "Somebody's Gotta Die," one of murdered rapper Notorious B.I.G.'s songs, he sang, "Retaliation for this one won't be minimal, cuz I'm a criminal . . . won't even know what happened, if it's done smoothly, silencers on the Uzi [submachine gun], somebody's gotta die." The band Rage Against the Machine screams repeatedly, "A bullet in ya head" in their song of the same name. Snoop Doggy Dogg threatens "187 on a [police officer]"—187 is the police radio code for a homicide. These are only a tiny fraction of the references to gun-fueled violence found in some of today's popular music lyrics.

Artists such as Pantera, 2 Live Crew, Dr. Dre, Marilyn Manson, N.W.A., Body Count, Cannibal Corpse, Eazy-E,

Ice-T, Tupac Shakur, Death, Venom, and Wasp are just a few of the performers who have written graphically violent lyrics.

The influence of violent lyrics and violent musicians on teens

In indisputable ways—how often violence appears, how explicit the description, the brutality toward women, the references to suicide and killing police—the violent lyrics in some of today's most popular music are more extreme than ever. However, there is continuing disagreement that greater levels of violence in music lyrics influence teens toward actual violence. Defenders tend to be popular music's listeners and producers, while the most vocal opponents include parent groups and some government leaders.

In response to opponents who say that teenagers are likely to emulate the violence portrayed in the song lyrics, defenders say that this best-selling music, rather than causing violence, simply reflects the level of violence encountered by teens growing up in the cities.

Christian activists often protest against the band Marilyn Manson, which has raised controversy, in part, for its depiction and glorification of satanic images.

54

Brian Warner of Marilyn Manson describes his violent lyrics as entertainment, but psychiatrists warn that too many negative images in the media can contribute to violent behavior among teens.

Other defenders of violent lyrics simply dismiss them as entertainment. Brian Warner, lead singer for Marilyn Manson, explained his "Kill your parents" song as theatrical entertainment for his huge concert audiences. This defense assumes that teenagers know the difference between reality and metaphor, and are capable of differentiating between real life and the tough verbal posturing of young musicians.

Although there have been stories in the papers describing isolated instances of "copy-cat" violence where a young person claimed the idea came from a movie or cartoon (for instance, the seventeen-year-old who blew himself up after learning from a *MacGyver* episode how to make a simple bomb and the youths who were killed after lying down on the center strip of a highway in imitation of a scene in the Disney movie *The Program),* there are no proven examples of music-inspired violence among youth.

Perhaps the pendulum of self-regulation in the commercial music industry has indeed swung to an extreme of explicit violence, as well as conspicuous sex and blatant bad taste. Does this necessarily mean that the teens who listen are likely to emulate what they hear and see? The debate on this question rages on, but, according to the AACAP, music is usually not a danger for a teenager whose life is happy and healthy. Music with seriously destructive and negative themes holds no interest for most kids, but the psychiatrists warn that the more negative music is, the more it may contribute to harmful behavior in conjunction with alcohol or other drug abuse, depression, and social isolation.

Society's reaction to violent lyrics in music

Under pressure from parent groups and government leaders, in the late 1980s the music industry began voluntarily placing music warning labels that express caution; for example, "Parental discretion advised," "Explicit lyrics," and "Some may find the lyrics offensive." The effectiveness of these warnings has been questioned. In some cases, it has appeared that the warnings actually serve as successful advertisements for violent music.

Besides opposition from parent groups and government leaders, most notably former senator and presidential candidate Bob Dole, violence in music is running into resistance from some parts of the music industry. For example, Moby Disc Records, a seven-store music retail chain in Southern California, has a strict policy of no-sale-to-minors of any music that appears on their list of artists producing violent or other controversial work. Furthermore, many urban radio stations with large teenage audiences like KMEL-FM in San Francisco have instituted voluntary policies of refusing to play songs with explicitly violent lyrics.

Ice Cube's contribution to movies and rap lyrics has been criticized for glamorizing violence and gang warfare.

Resistance to curtailing violent lyrics

Like other forms of entertainment that offend some segments of society, music with violent lyrics is generally protected by the First Amendment. Furthermore, it may be argued that the violence in music lyrics is either fictional or based on real events in the communities where the listeners live and as such does not instigate violence, a condition that might remove violent lyrics from the category of free speech.

Though many parents and other adults are shocked by the violent themes found in gangsta rap and rock music, some members of the AACAP have argued that these themes are symbols of some normal parts of growing up. The possibility of violence often shows up in a young person's struggle for independence and personal power. It is possible, say AACAP psychiatrists, that the violence in music lyrics encourages teenagers to confront the important ideas surrounding personal independence earlier than they might otherwise do.

Different viewpoints

Despite passionate declarations from people and organizations with different viewpoints, the role that media violence plays in teen violence remains unclear and unproven. Clearly, a considerable amount depends on parental supervision, but even that is a source of disagreement.

Some parents allow their children to be unfiltered—that is, the children can watch whatever they like. These parents believe they cannot forever prevent their children from watching and listening to what they want, and they believe that trying to screen their children from reality is not a desirable goal. In a 1996 article in the *San Diego Union-Tribune,* an eighteen-year-old high school girl's father, a counselor and instructor in a community college, said, "I've never gotten into the protection mode." The girl's mother added, "I didn't want her seeing things that were violent or sexual, but then she would go over to other people's houses and see R-rated or scary movies, and they didn't bother her. We trust her to use her good judgment. . . . If you make decisions for them, how can they learn to live in the world?"

Of course not all parents and child advocates agree with the unfiltered approach. "Young children absolutely need to be protected from media violence," said Victoria Rideout in the same *San Diego Union-Tribune* article. Rideout was speaking as the director of the children and media program for the Children Now advocacy organization. She believes that parents have to carefully study movie reviews, limit exposure to television violence, and enforce their perspectives as parents.

An unresolved question

Aside from which approach parents advocate, experts still do not agree on whether violent entertainment leads its audience to behave more violently. It is very likely, however, that whatever influence media violence wields upon American youth, it will never match the real-life violent atmosphere surrounding many of today's youth.

4

Gang Violence

GANG MEMBERS, GANGBANGERS, Original Gang-sters. The public's image of violent youth is, more often than not, the image of gangs. There is little doubt that a gang member lives with more real and threatened violence than an average teen, but just how much of the growth in teen violence is the result of gang activities? According to the U.S. Department of Justice, no one really knows.

The U.S. Justice Department's Office of Juvenile Justice and Delinquency Prevention (OJJDP) reports that police records on what appear to be gang incidents do not provide enough data to distinguish gang-related violence from other youth violence. Even though many reports indicate that new gangs and "franchises" of established gangs are appearing in more and more cities and towns, and that violence attributed to gangs is increasing, it remains unclear how much of the growth in urban youth violence is due to gangs, and how much is due to nongang teens or young adults. The result is that gang violence can only be discussed in terms of estimates, trends, and specific local examples that may or may not be representative of gang violence in all areas.

Yet, the large number of admitted and confirmed gang members being adjudicated for violent offenses in the courts has revealed a startling and crucial fact that has been verified by a number of research studies: only a very small number of teens commit the majority of violent crimes, and it appears very likely that most of those few belong to gangs.

Definition of a gang

For generations authorities and news reports have ascribed a large variety of violent criminal activities to gangs, also known as posses and crews. The truth, however, is that it is difficult to know how much teen violence is really attributable to gangs, despite their visibility and their proven involvement in violent activities.

What is actually meant by the term *gang*? According to a 1994 review of all of the available studies of American gangs prepared by James C. Howell for the OJJDP, there is no nationwide, government-accepted, standard definition of a gang. That means that, depending on who is speaking, a gang might be a large club with different branches and locations, a small neighborhood clique, a violent criminal ring, a drug-distribution business, or a combination of some or all of these descriptions.

The majority of teens that do commit violent crimes are involved in gang activities. These teen gang members are being questioned by police in Los Angeles.

Without a consistent definition of what constitutes a gang, it is impossible to accurately measure the violence committed by gang members. Since different law enforcement agencies across the country have different definitions for a gang, there is no consistent national reporting system of gang activity. As a result, no one really knows for sure how many gangs there are and how many members they have.

Sociologists have noted that unlike adult crime, most juvenile offenses are committed in groups. Therefore it is necessary to distinguish gangs from nongang groups of lawbreaking teenagers. Though the federal government is reluctant to give a standard definition, police, social service agencies, and researchers have developed their own criteria for what makes up a gang.

Police departments with gang units (most big-city departments), social service agencies, and research programs that investigate gangs have generally used some form of the following five criteria to define a gang: (1) there is a formal organizational structure; (2) there is identifiable leadership; (3) there is a specific territory considered by the members to be their turf; (4) there is frequent, regular interaction between members; and (5) members engage in criminal acts and violent behavior.

Speaking at a graduation ceremony in Los Angeles in 1996, Edward James Olmos, an actor nominated for an Academy Award for his performance in *Stand and Deliver,* defined a gang as a group whose members share similar interests and stand up for each other. By that definition, everyone belongs to some form of gang, even though some are called fraternities and clubs. Olmos noted that banding together and forming a group for mutual support is a normal human endeavor, but the activities of these groups become self-defeating when they include lethal violence. "Being in a gang is not bad in itself," said Olmos. "It is what you choose to do in the gang that is important."

American gangs today

Though the Department of Justice feels that its statistics on gangs are far from perfect, their 1993 survey of law

Actor Edward James Olmos feels teens naturally band together in groups for mutual support, not to engage in violence or illegal activities.

enforcement agencies using at least three of the five gang-definition criteria attempted to count the number of gangs operating in the United States. That survey of 1992 statistics produced a count of approximately 4,880 groups that matched the gang criteria. The membership at that time was about 250,000. By 1996, the OJJDP's National Youth Gang Center, still using "unofficial" criteria, counted 23,000 gangs with anywhere from 500,000 to perhaps 665,000 members nationwide.

The age of gang members, according to the OJJDP, ranges from about twelve to twenty-five years. The average age is seventeen. In some cities 90 percent of gang members are juveniles; in other cities only 25 percent are juveniles.

According to gang expert Malcolm Klein, in 1995 youth gangs were active in 125 American cities. Chicago alone has more than 100 gangs with an estimated 12,000 to 15,000 members. Estimates of the number of gangs in the Los Angeles area vary wildly—as low as 300 to as high as 950. As inconsistent and unreliable as nationwide gang data are, many cities have reported one estimate with uncharacteristic consistency: about 7 percent of all inner-city juveniles are gang members.

Other studies have attempted to determine how long a juvenile remains in a gang. Incarcerated gang members have reported being involved in gang life an average of five years. Being imprisoned for serious violent and drug crimes has generally been taken as evidence that most of these were hard-core gang members. When the OJJDP looked at all the members of selected street gangs, however, a different picture emerged. The surprising, though incomplete, finding was that although some hard-core members are active in gang life from early adolescence to their late twenties, more than half of the juveniles that become involved in a gang remain involved for no more than one year. The reasons for these short "enlistments" have yet to be carefully studied.

In a 1993 study of Hispanic gangs in Los Angeles by Richard Cervantes, 12 percent of the gang members reported that their fathers had been involved in gangs. Furthermore, Cervantes found that 54 percent had brothers in gangs, and 26 percent had a sister involved in a gang at some time.

Female gang members

Female membership in gangs also appears to be increasing, according to OJJDP reports. The OJJDP reported that in 1993, about 7,000 girls were members of gangs, about 3 percent of all gang members. Like all gang statistics, law enforcement officials have a difficult time estimating the number of girls in gangs. The Los Angeles Sheriff's Gang Enforcement Team reported in 1994 that they have files on about 100,000 active gang members and about 10 percent of them are girls. Are there 7,000 girl gang members in the country or 10,000 girl gang members in L.A. alone? The difficulties in defining and estimating gang membership frequently produce such disparate figures. But whichever figures are closest to the truth, one fact is clear: female membership in gangs is also increasing.

Ethnic composition

The racial and ethnic composition of gangs changes over time. Until the mid-1950s, the majority of gangs in the United States were made up of white immigrant adults and kids. By the 1970s, about 80 percent of gang members were either African American or Hispanic. Beginning in the 1980s, the growing focus on gangs produced numerous sets of statistics concerning ethnic composition that were seldom in agreement. For example, the Justice Department's OJJDP reported in 1990 that 55 percent of gang membership was African American and 33 percent was Hispanic. A year later the National Institute of Justice released its own figures, which indicated that 47.8 percent of gang members were African American, 42.7 percent were Hispanic, 5.2 percent were Asian, and 4.4 percent were white.

While the figures on ethnic gang membership vary from survey to survey, and while they may reflect a disproportionate focus on ethnic minority youths by police, they nevertheless point to a serious gang problem in ethnic communities.

Functions of gangs

Most gang members, regardless of their gender or race, come from poverty-stricken neighborhoods where fathers are frequently absent and mothers struggle to make a living, leaving children to fend for themselves. As a result, gangs, posses, and crews frequently serve as a kind of alternative family structure. It has even been suggested that gangs provide the discipline that all young people really long for but are not getting at home.

The picture of gang activities that emerges from the vast number of studies of gang life shows that gang members spend most of their time engaging in behavior that is not

Gang members recognize each other through styles of dress and hand signals. This member of the Los Angeles–based Big Hazard gang demonstrates his gang's sign in front of a memorial to dead members.

all that unusual among nongang adolescents. The most common gang activities appear to be hanging out, listening to music, cruising in a car, and drinking or getting high (though some gangs have taboos on taking addictive drugs). Add fighting and marking their turf with graffiti (tagging) and most of the activities of most gangs are covered. But it is no misconception that some gang members commit serious violent crimes in the course of their gang activities.

From interviews with violent gang members who were about to be tried as adults because of the brutality and magnitude of their crimes, a consistent psychological profile emerged that depicts what happens in gangs. The interviews revealed that gangs draw young people into a sort of aggressive but close-knit family that provides what the teens do not find at home—support, guidance, identity, and even a rough form of affection.

In most inner-city communities, interpersonal aggression is a fact of life. In this social environment, earning and keeping the respect of one's peers governs every aspect of public behavior, even violence. On the streets of the inner city, the need to build respect is directly linked to the need to be safe. The catch is that the test of being worthy of respect is usually violence. A young person lacking gang affiliation is in great danger of being tested during every outing.

Use of violence in gangs

Gangs meet a universal set of needs among young people, particularly the desire to feel important, to find excitement, and to have the material things they want. Gangs offer protection and acceptance to many teenagers who have no security or real family life, and gangs meet the fundamental human yearning to belong. This need often matters more to a poor kid than what must be done to gain admittance to and acceptance in a gang. To join a gang, a youngster has to be constantly tough, has to revenge every insult or sign of disrespect, has to carry a gun or a knife, and, sooner or later, has to use it.

The tools of violence used by gangs include fists and feet, bats, knives, and guns from simple revolvers to military-style automatic assault weapons. Violence intended to be less than lethal, although sometimes it goes too far, includes initiation and "jump-out" (the opposite of initiation—when a member wants out) beatings. These typically involve three to five members beating a new (or departing) member for three minutes, often leaving the victim unconscious and in dire need of hospital treatment. Even after being jumped-out the former member will be beaten again if gang members encounter him alone on the street. Sometimes the beatings end in death.

Intentionally lethal violence has become acceptable in many gangs. A gang member may be requested, pressured, or forced to use a gun for a variety of reasons, including to revenge an insult, to earn respect by demonstrating "nerve" and manliness, to avenge—often with a drive-by shooting—

a violent attack by members of a rival gang, or even sometimes in a random act of violence just for excitement.

Largely as a result of extensive media coverage, drive-by shootings are the kind of violence for which gangs are most infamous. In his 1992 report on gang crime, Los Angeles district attorney Ira Reiner said that drive-by shootings are typically committed by small sets of gang members, not entire gangs. In Reiner's analysis, drive-by shootings are most often related to revenge, turf disputes, and status. He described a long-running battle between two different sets of L.A.'s Crips that started over a junior high school romance. The result was a series of revenge drive-by shootings that produced over twenty deaths.

Lethal violence is usually the province of male gang members, but in violent gangs the females are not exempt from fighting and other forms of violence. Initiation, for example, can involve either surviving a timed beating or submitting to multiple rapes.

Most inner-city gang members develop a fearlessness that reflects the code of the streets. They do not back down. They are persistent in revenging an insult. They are obsessive in paying back an assault. And they fully expect that they could die violently at any time. Furthermore, they feel they have little to lose and much respect and reputation to gain by going to prison, so they are not concerned with police or the law. When gang members reach the point where they have no fear, no hope for real jobs, and no stake in the system, they often cut all their ties to mainstream society.

Relationship between gang violence and drugs

A great deal of publicity has been generated about the use of lethal violence by some gangs to control drug business, particularly the distribution of crack cocaine in cities. Research, however, has provided little evidence that most inner-city teen homicides are the result of drug-related violence.

Work by Malcolm Klein with gangs in Los Angeles from the mid-1980s to the mid-1990s, as well as reports from other research, found that gang members were involved in only about a quarter of the arrests for crack distribution, and they were arrested for less than 10 percent of the drug-related homicides. Klein reported that even though 25 percent of crack distribution arrests were of gang members, only certain gang members were heavily involved and drug trafficking was not the primary activity in most violent gangs.

A study of Chicago gangs reported by OJJDP appears to verify Klein's work. The OJJDP study found that of the city's four largest and most criminally active street gangs, only 8 of 285 gang-motivated homicides between 1987 and 1990 were related to drugs. In the Boston area, police reports indicate that only about 10 percent of the violent crimes committed by gang members involved drug dealing

Although gang violence more often erupts over competition for territory than drug-related issues, some gang members do participate in drug distribution.

or use of drugs. A few drug trafficking gangs, cliques within gangs, and gangs organized exclusively for drug distribution have been identified, but research clearly indicates that far more gang violence occurs as the result of intergang competition for turf.

Signs of change

In the past, police have responded to gang violence with military-like attacks, and the courts have thrown tens of thousands of gang members into prisons. Nevertheless as gang violence continued to escalate, inner-city neighborhoods and housing projects began condemning the violence and striving to provide alternatives to gang life for their youth. Then local and state governments started forming task forces to create prevention programs that draw upon members of the communities, service organizations, police, and schools.

There is a new consensus that prevention offers the best chance of diverting teens from a dead-end life. Many people now see the violent actions of gang members as symptoms of a community's problems like substandard schools, joblessness, boredom, dysfunctional families, intense poverty, and despair. The hope is that prevention will prove to be successful in directing a community's energies toward solving these problems and providing meaningful alternatives to gang life.

Beginning in 1994, signs began to appear that gangs were using less violence. For example, in that year the Bloods and the Crips, the two notorious gangs based in Los Angeles, agreed to a truce, which produced a significant drop in gang violence in Southern California. Then the 1995 crime figures from the FBI showed the first decline in gang-related violence in more than ten years.

5

Teens in the Juvenile Justice System

FOR MOST OF the twentieth century, Americans' response to teen violence has leaned heavily toward reacting to it rather than preventing it. In the face of shrill headlines about exploding teen violence, government at all levels has tended to pour ever-increasing amounts of money into more police, more law enforcement hardware, more prisons, and more courts. Since the 1980s, expenditures in the United States for criminal justice (juvenile and adult combined) have increased four times as rapidly as for education and twice as rapidly as for health and hospitals, according to the Milton S. Eisenhower Foundation, which studies inner-city crime.

There are hundreds of different laws, police strategies, and community programs to deter teen violence, but when deterrence fails the juvenile justice system takes over.

The juvenile justice system

The first juvenile court was established in 1899 in Cook County, Illinois, and by 1925 forty-six states had juvenile courts. Today 95 percent of juvenile crime is handled by the state courts and only 5 percent by the federal government. For most of the twentieth century, the goal of the juvenile justice system has been rehabilitation, unlike the adult justice system, which is based on accountability and punishment. Juveniles could not be held accountable for wrongdoing because, the argument went, they were too

The goal of the juvenile justice system is not only to punish but also to educate. Classes such as the one shown here in a Los Angeles youth prison help to rehabilitate gang members and other teen offenders.

young to understand the consequences of their actions and to show mature judgment. Criminal behavior in juveniles was seen as a sort of youthful illness that could be cured with the right combination of counseling, teaching, and role modeling.

The emphasis on treatment and rehabilitation is still reflected in the words used in juvenile justice. People below the age of eighteen who commit crimes are not criminals but delinquents. Instead of being arrested, they are "taken into custody," where they are detained rather than jailed. Instead of being charged with a crime, they are referred to the court where they have a hearing, not a trial. They are not convicted and sentenced—they are found delinquent and placed, not imprisoned, in a residential facility, a detention center, or a juvenile work camp.

A new mood in juvenile justice

Starting in the 1970s, state governments, prompted by the public's concern over widespread reports of drastic increases in violent juvenile crime, enacted laws designed to change the authority and practice of the juvenile justice system. These laws, though they varied greatly from state to state and continue to do so, sought to alter three basic aspects of juvenile justice: reducing or removing the confidentiality of juvenile records, reducing the power of juvenile court judges to consider the future welfare of young offenders, and requiring longer, tougher punishments for violent juveniles.

The trend toward uncompromising treatment of violent juveniles accelerated in the late 1980s after a series of Department of Justice reports revealed that juvenile homicide rates were climbing even though the teenage population was not growing. The states responded with tougher laws that forced courts to prosecute violent teenagers the same as violent adults and punish them with imprisonment instead of attempting to rehabilitate them. Consequently, the latest version of the juvenile justice system is quite different in appearance from the system that was in place before 1970.

The wave of legislation that swept through the juvenile justice system between 1970 and 1990 has effectively dismantled much of the treatment-oriented system that tended to put violent teenage offenders back on the streets. As a result, violent and habitual juvenile criminals are now far more likely to receive long-term incarceration (lockup) instead of treatment or probation. In many states that means the more violent teens are treated as adult criminals. Furthermore, there is much less willingness on the part of state legislatures to provide funding for rehabilitation activities (education, drug counseling, job training) during incarceration.

Confidentiality of juvenile records is fast becoming extinct

For decades, records of juvenile crime have been treated with special confidentiality to keep a rehabilitated teenager's mistakes from interfering with later activities like getting a job. As a result, juvenile records were usually sealed, a practice that made it difficult or even impossible years later for courts and law enforcement agencies to determine if a person they had arrested was a first offender or a habitual criminal.

Faced with large numbers of far more serious juvenile offenders than the legislators had in mind when they created the confidentiality laws, most states have passed new laws that remove much of the protected status once conferred on teens by their age. The increased seriousness of juvenile violence created a need to share information about teen offenders between law enforcement agencies so they could better protect the public. In prosecuting violent adult offenders, it had become more important than ever to know if they had violent juvenile records. Consequently, a demand arose to make juvenile arrest records, court proceedings, and sentences open to all law enforcement agencies and courts. New laws and procedures have made it far more difficult for young adult criminals to leave their juvenile records behind them.

Where crime and punishment meet: the juvenile court

The juvenile court plays a critical role in the lives of children and teens who enter its workings. When juveniles are arrested and charged with a serious crime, they are adjudicated—that is, placed under the jurisdiction of the juvenile court. Since there are no jury trials in the juvenile justice system, their immediate fate is in the hands of the judge.

When a teenager is brought into court and accused of a violent offense, the judge usually orders immediate or continued detention to protect the public from further delinquent acts. At a subsequent hearing, the judge then hears testimony from police and witnesses and reports from probation officers before deciding the offender's fate. The brutality of the crime and the teenager's history will influence the judge's decision. First offenders may receive probation, which means being released under the supervision of a court-appointed probation officer with the condition that the juvenile maintain good behavior. Whenever possible, the offenders are released into the custody of their parents; this is provided as an alternative to incarceration for some teenagers provided, of course, that they have no record of serious crime.

For serious and repeat offenders, the option of probation does not exist. These teenagers are most likely to be sentenced to juvenile hall, reform school, youth ranch, work

Instead of waiting for jury trials, the fate of juvenile offenders is decided immediately by a judge. First-time offenders are often appointed probation officers to whom they must report periodically.

camp, boot camp, or a youth prison. In cases of serious violence or habitual criminality, adjudication can also result in a waiver, meaning the juvenile is transferred into adult court and prosecuted as an adult criminal. Sentencing as an adult is done to remove the possibility of a violent teen's getting off with a relatively short sentence. Many states allow judges to decide on a case-by-case basis whether to waive a sixteen-year-old offender. In two states children as young as ten can be waived to adult courts, and several states have no minimum age at all.

From juvenile to adult court

The OJJDP's juvenile court statistics show that the number of cases (nationwide) transferred to criminal adult court by waiver grew by 29 percent between 1987 and 1991, from about seven thousand cases to about nine thousand cases, and the number of waived cases continued to increase through 1997. Nevertheless, the success of waivers in punishing offenders and deterring crime is questionable. The National Council on Crime and Delinquency (NCCD) has observed that waiver to adult court often leads to dismissal, reduced charges, or probation rather than incarceration in adult prisons, although this may be changing. Furthermore, several states have had their violent juvenile arrest rates actually increase following the introduction of waivers (New York, Idaho, and Florida, according to the NCCD). In fact, Florida has relied extensively on mandatory waiver and yet that state suffers from one of the nation's most serious juvenile violent crime problems.

Depending on the state, there are several degrees of consequences for violent juvenile offenders. The most severe is waiver to adult court, sentencing as an adult, and imprisonment in adult institutions along with the adult inmates. Then there is "graduated incarceration," where juveniles are kept in juvenile correctional facilities until they turn eighteen, at which time they may be transferred to adult facilities for the remainder of their sentence. A few states attempt to keep some of the old approach to juvenile justice

by sentencing their violent juveniles to "segregated incarceration," where they are housed in separate facilities with other juveniles with the possibility of qualifying for special training, boot camps, or rehabilitation programs.

Of the approximately 1 million individuals locked up in all types of prisons in the United States, about seventy-five thousand are teenagers. Locking up violent juveniles is expensive. The New York State Division for Youth, which keeps juvenile offenders in large institutions, reports that it spends about $30,000 per year per individual. The National Council on Crime and Delinquency puts the figure at between $35,000 and $60,000 per year to incarcerate one juvenile in a state reform school (called training schools in some states). That is more than the annual tuition at some of the country's best private colleges.

These Los Angeles gang members are segregated from other teens in a juvenile prison cell. In addition to segregation, violent offenders may also be transferred to adult facilities.

Questions about more and longer prison terms for juveniles

The drop in the national crime rates that occurred in 1995 followed a dramatic increase in the number of offenders of all ages sentenced to long prison terms during the 1980s and 1990s. Putting more people in prison certainly leads to less crime—at least for a while. Incarceration keeps violent offenders off the streets for years, but some organizations question whether locking up more people, particularly juveniles, is effective in reducing crime rates. The National Council on Crime and Delinquency points out that even though the American prison population doubled between 1980 and 1990, serious crime, including violent juvenile crime, decreased in the mid-1990s an average of less than 20 percent. Clearly locking up more violent offenders does have some effect on reducing crime, but more than 80 percent of the crimes continue unabated.

Everyone in the juvenile justice system agrees that juveniles who have committed brutal crimes of violence should be incarcerated to punish them and protect the public. As a deterrent to crime, longer and tougher prison sentences seem to reduce violent juvenile crime in some states while such sentences are largely ineffective in others (most notably in Florida). The American Academy of Child and Adolescent Psychiatry cites numerous studies showing that teenagers seldom think about consequences when they are tempted by the peer pressure and excitement of street crime and gang membership. This might explain why tougher sentencing practices are not as effective in deterring violent crime as legislators hoped they would be.

The policy of sending increasing numbers of individuals to prison has had some startling consequences. According to statistics from the National Council on Crime and Delinquency, by the early 1990s the United States had a far higher percentage of its population in prison than any other industrialized nation in the world. In California and several other states, more money was spent on prisons in 1996 than on education.

Furthermore, the increase in numbers of people incarcerated has not occurred at the same rate for all races. Figures from the 1991 U.S. Census Bureau's Children in Custody Survey show that black juveniles are confined in facilities at over three times the rate of white juveniles and Hispanic juveniles are confined at a rate 60 percent greater than that of whites. In 1995, a third of all black American males were under arrest, in jail or prison, on probation, or on parole. Aside from the frequently asserted idea that these statistics are related to deep-seated racism, the fact remains (documented in NCCD and OJJDP studies) that minority youth, particularly African Americans, are almost twice as likely to be held in secure pretrial confinement than are white youth. Similarly, minority youth in the United States consistently receive more severe dispositions than white youth and are more likely to be committed to state institutions than whites for the same offenses.

Black juveniles make up the greatest percentage of incarcerated teens and often receive harsher sentencing than other teens who commit the same crimes.

Because of poverty, the families of minority youths are often unable to arrange for the same kind of strong legal representation more generally possible for white families. The free legal counsel supplied in some courts is often inadequate—Mary Broderick, director of the National Legal Aid and Defender Association, noted that juvenile court is frequently used as a training ground for inexperienced public defenders.

The changes in how violent juvenile offenders are sentenced, the increase in prosecution of violent juvenile offenders as adults, and the opening of juvenile offenders' records will, according to the OJJDP, have a disproportionate impact on minority teens because they are already overrepresented in the serious and violent crime categories. The judicial trend that began in the 1970s is propelling more minority juvenile offenders into adult courts and prison systems than nonminority offenders.

Despite the move toward longer sentences for juveniles, the traditional views of juvenile justice are still alive. Since the majority of juvenile offenders are involved in less serious wrongdoing, much of the juvenile justice system continues to be guided by the belief that, given a chance, a troubled young person will usually change for the better. Nevertheless, treating increasing numbers of both violent and nonviolent juveniles as adult criminals represents a fundamental shift in America's juvenile justice philosophy, a shift that reflects the increasingly brutal acts of a small percentage of teenage offenders.

Moving violent teens into the adult justice system

Responding to overwhelming evidence that less than 15 percent of juvenile offenders commit 50 to 75 percent of the serious violent juvenile crime, the OJJDP created the Serious Habitual Offender Comprehensive Action Program (SHOCAP). SHOCAP is a federal program designed to help law enforcement and justice systems at the state level, where most juvenile prosecution takes place, identify, track, arrest, and prosecute the most violent juvenile offenders. One outcome of SHOCAP is that more violent and habitual offenders are being prosecuted as adult criminals.

Talking about the most brutal juveniles in a 1992 speech, William P. Barr, the U.S. attorney general at the time, stated: "Every experienced law enforcement officer has encountered 16- and 17-year-olds who are as mature and criminally hardened as adult offenders. Public safety demands that these habitual and dangerous criminals be tried and punished as adults."

Like other advocates of a tougher criminal justice system for young offenders, the former attorney general and the OJJDP believe that too many violent teenagers have escaped significant punishment, and that this has created the prevailing attitude among juvenile offenders that they will face no serious punishment for illegal behavior. That may be changing since the juvenile justice system has started frequently using the waiver to adult court.

While the legal basis for waiver varies from state to state, the clear trend is a rapid increase in the use of waiver. By the mid-1990s, almost every state had passed legislation lowering the age of adult jurisdiction and increasing the number of offenses that could be transferred to adult court. Most states now also require that juveniles with a repetitive criminal history be waived to adult criminal court.

Are long sentences ineffective?

The wisdom of moving large numbers of teen offenders into the adult justice system has been challenged by many groups, including, surprisingly enough, the Department of Justice. The department stated in its 1996 report on violent juvenile crime, "The violent criminal behavior of a relatively small proportion of juvenile offenders has created a public perception of rampant violent crime by juveniles." The report expressed concern that many of the new laws that were sending more juveniles into the adult system were written following emotionally charged, political speeches that passionately urged action to "curb juvenile violence." In some instances, a single sensational incident

The 'Get Tough on Crime' frenzy reaches an obvious climax...

prompted a new law. The report noted that although some states had succeeded in making their juvenile justice systems more punitive, more costly, and more like their adult counterparts, the evidence for a decrease in juvenile violence was inconclusive.

Opponents of treating violent juvenile offenders as adults and giving them long sentences in adult correctional institutions point to research showing that involvement in serious violent crime peaks between age sixteen and seventeen. According to the National Council on Crime and Delinquency, high-risk juveniles do not remain high-risk. Criminologists have established that the likelihood of violent teens' continuing to commit crimes of violence after the age of twenty drops dramatically. A 1988 study by the

California Department of Youth Authority concluded that longer sentences for youthful offenders have little or no impact on crime and public safety.

Some states have attempted to strike a balance between punishing juvenile offenders, protecting the public, restoring a sense of community in violence-torn areas, and enhancing offenders' chances of eventually becoming law-abiding, contributing members of society. These attempts at balance include isolating the serious habitual offenders from other juveniles by applying SHOCAP techniques and transferring them to the adult system, increasing funding of job training, youth programs, and family community services, and establishing rehabilitation and supervision programs for first offenders. The type and length of punishment a violent teen receives varies from state to state, so there is no uniform, nationwide approach.

Small institutions for the small percentage

A 1994 report by the National Council on Crime and Delinquency has named three states—Massachusetts, Utah, and Missouri—as having the closest to what it considers to be model youth corrections systems for violent juvenile offenders. Each of these states has abandoned large reform schools and developed small, secure facilities for the few juveniles (about 15 percent) who are dangerous. The largest of these facilities holds twenty teenagers. The vast majority of nonviolent juvenile offenders are placed in group homes, foster care, day treatment programs, and intensive supervision programs at less cost. Furthermore, with these programs Massachusetts and Utah transfer very few teens to adult criminal courts.

The National Council on Crime and Delinquency points out that the purpose of programs like these is to increase the effectiveness of juvenile justice, not to save money. The money not spent on large training schools goes into the small but intensive serious offender programs and extensive follow-up efforts.

Evaluation of the Massachusetts and Utah juvenile systems shows that offenders who went through them were

significantly less likely to commit violent crimes after release than graduates of large reform schools and detention
facilities. The Massachusetts program began in 1970, and
so far the major juvenile crime wave predicted by skeptics
has not occurred.

Alternatives to putting juveniles behind bars for years

Department of Justice statistics show that 94 percent of
young prisoners with extensive records of serious and violent crime are arrested again within three years of release.
The New York State Division for Youth reports that 65
percent of all its juvenile prisoners are arrested again after
they are released. Figures like these are used to support
the argument that locking up teens is only a short-term solution to deterring violent crime. Opponents of the quick
fix solution argue that these former juvenile offenders go
right back to their old ways, often because they have no
education, job training, or hope for a life in mainstream
America.

Fearing that many juveniles incarcerated for violent acts
will become repeat offenders when they are released, many
states are looking for alternatives to locking teenagers up
in prisons, alternatives that may help teens build the matu-
rity and skills needed to leave their violent actions behind
them and to join mainstream society. Behind this search
for alternatives is the idea that there is still some hope for
these teenagers.

A common alternative to juvenile hall and prison-style
facilities is the juvenile ranch, or work camp. Most work
camps have no walls or locked doors, and counselors and
work group leaders replace guards. Found in secluded locations in every state, these facilities do not represent new
alternatives, but the way they are run has changed in recent
years. In the ranches and camps, life is highly structured
and almost all the time is filled with work, counseling,
school, and health programs. The core message drummed
into young offenders at these places is "Take charge of
your life."

The primary incentive for offenders to gain control of their lives is the fear of prison. The courts and the counselors inform teens who are sent to work camps or ranches that if they do not follow the rules, the next stop is prison.

This privately run work camp in South Carolina provides an alternative to prison for convicted juvenile offenders.

For many of the kids at juvenile ranches and camps, violence has been a large part of their lives, and it is hard to shake their old ways. Many do fairly well while they are under close supervision, but the statistics show that over half of them get back into trouble after they are released from ranches and camps. In an attempt to remedy this, the juvenile justice system is placing more emphasis on better postrelease supervision and continued drug and alcohol treatment to help the teenagers who want to stay sober.

Boot camp

Another alternative to prison for youthful violent offenders is what has come to be known as boot camp, named after the tough, disciplined training camp through which all new military recruits pass. Some states call their boot camps "shock incarceration." Though tougher than work ranches and camps, these facilities are also seen as a final rehabilitation opportunity for teenagers who otherwise would be serving time in prison. With the alternative being a one-to-two-year prison sentence, most offenders who are offered a ninety-day boot camp gladly accept.

Offenders typically spend their time in boot camp undergoing intense physical and disciplinary training designed to teach them that they are ultimately responsible for their actions. Often the boot camps are located within the walls of prisons so the young offenders are constantly reminded of what awaits them if they do not get the message. After three months, they are released on parole.

A drill instructor reprimands a juvenile offender at the medium-security Second Chance Boot Camp in Washington State.

A more extreme version of a boot camp is the Florida Environmental Institute (FEI). Opened in 1982, FEI houses some of Florida's most violent youth, and it does so without fences, lockdowns, or the physical restraints usually associated with maximum-security programs. Located in a remote area of the northern reaches of the Florida Everglades, FEI is surrounded by swamps and forests. The facilities are wooden structures built by the inmates and staff. The program in the camp emphasizes hard work. After work, each teen receives counseling and attends classes. The typical amount of time spent at FEI is eighteen months.

Work ranches and camps, boot camps, and FEI have all demonstrated improvement in recidivism rates (going back to court for new crimes) on the order of 5 percent (average of 28 percent recidivism within one year after being released from prison versus 23 percent recidivism within one year after being released from a camp or ranch).

Growing pressure of demographics on juvenile justice

Demographics, the study of the composition and distribution of a population, reveals an approaching crisis in juvenile violence and fuels debate among people and agencies charged with administering juvenile justice. The sheer pressure of numbers has the courts and detention centers bulging at the seams. According to the U.S. Census Bureau, in 1980 there were about 10.7 million males in the fifteen- to nineteen-year-old age group (most violent juvenile crimes are committed by males). By 1990 there were only 9.2 million. But by 2010, projections indicate that there will be about 11.5 million fifteen- to nineteen-year-old males in the United States. Furthermore, it seems likely, based on what sociologists are seeing in impoverished inner-city families, that an unprecedented number of those teenagers will grow up in troubled homes and high-crime communities, both factors that tend to encourage violent behavior.

This prediction of such a large growth in the teen population squelched optimism about recent drops in violent juvenile crime levels. The growing concern and fear arising from the demographic predictions lend a sense of urgency to the debates over where to focus attention and funds in juvenile justice, crime prevention, law enforcement, and prison expansion.

Finding a better response to teen violence

No one disputes that the public has a right to be protected from violent criminals of all ages. But for every law enforcement expert like Los Angeles County district attorney Gil Garcetti, who insists that "if they are old enough to do the crime they are old enough to do the time," there is a group like the Coalition for Juvenile Justice arguing that locking up increasing numbers of young people has an enormous economic and social cost and will probably fail to have a lasting effect on reducing teen violence. In efforts to avoid the expense of incarcerating juvenile offenders, many social scientists and governmental agencies are turning to strategies for preventing teen violence.

6

Preventing Teen Violence

IN A MONUMENTAL effort to protect the public from dangerous teens, the government and the police of the United States have arrested, prosecuted, and imprisoned record numbers of juveniles, but the violence has continued. By the mid-1990s, all but the most battle-hungry police were willing to admit that harsh suppression of violent teens produced only local, temporary successes and that it was not working to quell urban violence over the long run. Law enforcement and the juvenile justice system were forced to look for other strategies for achieving long-term reductions in teen violence.

Even though violent juvenile crime declined somewhat between 1995 and 1997, locking up juveniles after they have already hurt or killed someone has not achieved the major reductions in juvenile violence that are needed. Furthermore, tougher laws and courts so far have produced disappointing results in preventing juvenile violence. Instead, government agencies and many levels of society have concluded that treating the causes of teen violence offers the best hope of preventing it.

The public health approach to preventing teen violence

The U.S. surgeon general has declared teen violence to be a public health issue like other health threats, for example, disease, tainted food, toxic wastes, and drugs.

According to the surgeon general's office, treating firearm injuries costs nearly $3 billion a year in medical expenses, and at least 20 percent of that cost is the result of teens shooting teens.

The health problems of violence are measured in more ways than direct medical cost. Dozens of studies document both the immediate and the long-term psychological and physical consequences of violence to victims, witnesses, and family members. Students at inner-city schools, for example, frequently show all the signs of post–traumatic stress disorder usually associated with combat veterans.

Prevention is the tried and proven response to controlling a public health hazard. Taking this approach, the U.S. surgeon general has said that to prevent teen violence, the risk of a child facing violence in the future must be reduced and the immediate sources of violence to adolescents and teens must be removed. Seen in the context of a public health problem, preventing teen violence is a long-term, coordinated effort involving not only teens but also their families, social attitudes, and neighborhoods.

Jim Borgman. Reprinted with special permission of King Features Syndicate.

Prevention starts in the family

A primary role of parents in any family is to maintain an orderly home environment that includes supervision and discipline. Lacking supervision and discipline, teens are apt to define the boundaries of their own behavior. Without guidance, juveniles may come to view violence as acceptable behavior. To help more teenagers in their needs for guidance, some community outreach programs are concentrating on teaching parents more effective parenting skills. These programs recognize that good parenting does not just happen, and it is even less likely in people who themselves have never experienced good parenting.

The qualities of good parenting are mostly learned, and therefore they can be taught. Advocates for children believe that the privilege and responsibilities of parenting should include learning how to do it right. That learning—what is sometimes called parenting training—is increasingly available to people from all walks of life.

A prime example of a good-parenting program is Healthy Families America, launched in 1992 by the Chicago-based nonprofit National Committee to Prevent Child Abuse in partnership with Ronald McDonald House Charities. Healthy Families America works with hospitals, prenatal clinics, and doctors to identify mothers in stressful and potentially abusive situations either before they give birth or immediately afterward. These women are provided with weekly home visits, counseling, and similar support for as long as five years. The only thing preventing nationwide adoption of this and similar programs is money. Healthy Families America costs up to $2,000 per family per year, most of which must come from local government sources.

One of the things that shows up the most frequently in the personal histories of violent teens is that they were, as young children, physically abused or neglected by one or both parents. Consequently child abuse prevention is now seen as a key to preventing teen violence. An example of a promising child abuse prevention program is Hawaii's Healthy Start, funded by the state since 1987. This program starts helping young and at-risk parents become good fathers and mothers the day their baby arrives. A caseworker interviews new parents in the hospital shortly after their child is born. The aim is to identify parents who may be at risk of abusing their children, which includes teen mothers, alcoholics, drug users, welfare recipients, or individuals who themselves have been abused either as children or adults. Parents who fall into the high-risk category are offered, at no charge, the services of a home visitor for up to five years. The home visitor shows parents how to feed and nurture a baby, and they ensure that children get regular, preventative medical care. In some cases they help parents find jobs and housing. Parents are not forced to enroll in the program, but few refuse. Hawaii's Healthy Start has been calculated to cost less than half of what the state spends each year on postabuse protective custody and foster care.

In 1996, the Rand Corporation released the results of a study that showed parenting training works. The study found that when trained health-care professionals pay regular visits to the home of new parents, who also receive parent training, there are significant reductions in problem behaviors of the children in those families in later years. Programs like Healthy Start are now functioning in every state. Though it is too early to measure their full effect, officials are optimistic that reducing the number of child abuse victims will cause a major drop in teen violence in the years to come.

The community as extended family

Successful community-based programs must provide multiple answers to multiple problems. For those that deal directly with teens, these programs must respond to a variety of young people who have different backgrounds and different problems by matching the amount and kind of support and discipline to each individual. They do this by linking mentors, counselors, and peers with teens who need help with school, job training, job placement, or solving personal problems. Many community-based programs act as an extended family by providing a supportive, nur-

turing, and disciplined place to go after school and on weekends. These are the conditions that are necessary for individual growth but are lacking in the lives of many of the young people served by these organizations.

Community-based violence prevention programs come in many forms, both private (business and charity supported) and public (government supported). These programs are generally grouped as job centered, counseling centered, and recreation centered, although most programs contain aspects of all three types.

Since the lack of decent jobs has been shown as one of the primary contributors to gang violence, violence prevention programs for older teens concentrate on preparing participants for work and helping them find jobs that offer the possibility for advancement and a chance to join the mainstream of American life. That is the mission of the Jobs Corps, JobStart, Project Redirection, and other examples of the job-centered approach to violence prevention.

Teens who feel needed and nurtured within the community are less likely to commit violent crimes. Groups like the Boys and Girls Clubs provide opportunities for teens to get involved.

Counseling-centered programs offer guidance in diverse areas including improving school performance, staying out of jail, getting out of gang life, getting off drugs and alcohol, resolving conflict in nonviolent ways, and solving personal problems. Omega in San Francisco, Phoenix in Akron, Ohio, and Argus in the south Bronx are just three of the many community-based counseling-centered programs around the country.

While there is little objective information about the success rates of job- and counseling-centered approaches to teen violence, there are volumes of personal success stories, and, of course, volumes of cases where these kinds of offered help were rejected. The general feeling among people involved in these programs is that even without clear-cut proof of their effectiveness, they are worth continuing because they are better than doing nothing and because in at least some cases they work.

The Boys and Girls Clubs

The primary recreation-centered teen violence prevention program is the Boys and Girls Clubs of America. Based primarily in urban areas, the Boys and Girls Clubs initially draw inner-city teens with recreational opportunities. Once inside, they are on neutral ground—no gang colors, no weapons. The result is that kids from different gangs, who had previously only faced each other in deadly turf wars, end up playing basketball and football together.

Each potential new member is welcomed and ushered into the regular activities by a club professional who takes a special interest in each youngster. Bonding between the teenager and an adult staff member is one of the most effective tools the club has to influence the life of a young person in a positive direction. The relationships between club adults and the new members may lead to, if needed, drug counseling, family therapy, or job training. This approach has turned so many teens away from gang life that in some areas judges often sentence teens to Boys and Girls Club programs rather than sending them to a lockup.

Escaping from the dangers and pressures of gang life requires the intensity of a multifaceted recreation and counseling program like the Boys and Girls Clubs because in areas of high gang activity, the violence can seem almost inescapable to a teen. In these areas not only are the streets violent, but so are the schools.

Violence prevention in schools

Teen violence in schools is a major problem because of its prevalence and because it disrupts the education process. To prevent violence in schools, education researchers have found that teachers and school staff must consistently show by their example that reasoning out or negotiating a solution to a problem will ultimately serve everyone better than violence. Research also indicates that school must not be treated as if it has different rules than

Children at the Boys and Girls Club in St. Paul, Minnesota, not only participate in recreational activities, but can also develop their educational skills.

Teenage Boys and Girls Club members attend special training classes to learn how to resist the pressures of alcohol, drugs, and premature sexual relations.

the rest of the community—what is illegal outside of school is illegal inside school, so all violent crimes including possession of weapons must be reported to the police.

Zero-tolerance

To enforce the community's laws inside the school, some school districts have introduced zero-tolerance policies for guns, drugs, and fighting. Zero-tolerance means immediate suspension for anyone caught carrying any weapon, drinking alcohol, using or dealing drugs, or fighting on campus. Even first offenders are suspended from school for a semester or more, depending on the seriousness of the offense. Strict, no-exception, zero-tolerance policies have been implemented by the Texas Safe Schools Act of 1995 and a number of other school districts around the country, and as a result all report drops in violent acts and threats against both students and teachers.

Reports indicate that vigorous enforcement of the zero-tolerance policy reduces campus violence by about 30 percent, but critics say such policies do not solve problems, they only push the violence and drug use into the neigh-borhoods around the schools. Furthermore, say critics of zero-tolerance, students who violate the policy and are sus-pended have no incentive to stop their criminal activities.

School uniforms as a violence prevention measure

Although kids do not seem to care much for the idea, school uniforms are attracting growing interest from public school administrators and parents as a way of preventing teen violence. According to supporters, the advantages of uniforms far outweigh any curtailment of individual rights that may be represented by the requirement.

Advocates of school uniforms say there are two ways that uniforms can reduce teen violence. One is that students will better be able to avoid the kind of trouble caused by showing gang colors and styles (whether on purpose or ac-cidentally) when they must pass through gang territories on the way to and from school. The other way is that uniforms

President Clinton, pictured here with a student from the Long Beach school district in California, supports school uniforms as a method of reducing teen violence at school.

allow for easy and immediate identification of outsiders (like older gang members) who do not belong on campus.

The first large public school system in the country to implement a mandatory school uniform policy was the Long Beach Unified School District (LBUSD), located at the southern boundary of Los Angeles. LBUSD was plagued by school violence caused mostly by gang rivalry. Frightened and disgusted by the increasing violence in and near the schools, twenty-five hundred parents and students joined together to demand, among other things, school uniforms. The district superintendent and the board of education responded with a mandatory uniform policy that went into effect in 1994. A preliminary evaluation conducted by the LBUSD after the first year indicated that school violence had dropped 36 percent.

Conflict resolution

Because serious violence has spread throughout so many schools, education experts nationwide have begun to insist that teachers and school administrators accept dealing with school violence as a vital part of education rather than an intrusion on it. Making the campus safe is absolutely necessary, but that is not enough. Teaching students to care about and to predict the consequences of their actions is the goal, so practicing and teaching options to violence, such as conflict resolution and peer mediation, must be a daily occurrence if violence in schools is to be halted.

Conflict resolution education has become one of the most heavily promoted areas of violence prevention in public schools. Conflict resolution is a group of skills, including negotiation, mediation, and decision making between two or more people, designed to allow the people involved in a conflict or disagreement to settle it in a nonviolent way. Conflict resolution can take a variety of forms, many of which have their own names (peer mediation, Positive Adolescent Choices Training, and Second Step, for example).

Peer mediation, where specially trained students help other students settle their differences peacefully, is sometimes better accepted by teens than other forms of conflict

resolution. Originally developed as a method of settling labor disputes, in recent years it has been used on school campuses and within community groups like the Boys and Girls Clubs.

In peer mediation, students volunteer to serve as referees (mediators) in conflicts between other teens. To be a peer mediator, a student must undergo several weeks of training. Peer mediation helps teens learn how to deal with common previolent situations like name-calling, shoving, and verbal threats. Part of the power and uniqueness of peer mediation is that no school staff members, parents, or police are present, nor is there any intervention or punishment from adults. The idea is for the students themselves to defuse these problems before they escalate into violence.

A teacher uses the popular Second Step Curriculum to teach her fourth- and fifth-grade students the social skills needed to refrain from violence.

School-based programs

Violence prevention programs in the schools are often intertwined with community-based violence prevention efforts. Recently there has been rapid growth in programs developed by nonprofit community organizations and businesses for teaching children and teens in school how to manage anger. One example is Positive Adolescent Choices Training (PACT) developed for middle and junior high school students by educators at Wright State University in Ohio. PACT programs are taught in health education classes, and their goal is to defuse violence by having students learn how to talk instead of fight.

PACT participants use role-playing to reenact the kinds of real-life disputes that can easily escalate into violence. They learn to talk about the issue with the people who have angered them, and they learn ways to move those talks toward nonviolent outcomes, agreements, and compromises.

Programs like PACT have more effect when parents are involved. Knowing that in some homes parents might be screaming at their children, throwing things at them, or threatening them, program designers developed IMPACT as a companion program for parents. IMPACT teaches parents how to control their anger and how to discipline their children in fair and effective ways. The program also helps parents understand what their children are feeling and the peer pressure they are facing.

Another violence prevention curriculum for middle school children is Second Step, developed by the Seattle-based, nonprofit Committee for Children. This program is designed to teach children to avoid or change the attitudes and behaviors that lead to violence. The curriculum is based on extensive research into the very social skills that are lacking in people with violent tendencies: empathy, impulse control, problem solving, and anger management.

Preliminary evaluations by several school boards of school-based violence prevention programs like PACT and

Second Step indicate that they are often successful at reducing violent behavior, but the programs vary widely in consistency and how well they are taught.

Yet, conflict resolution is considered to be such a powerful tool for reducing violence that U.S. attorney general Janet Reno directed the Department of Justice to develop a national program for conflict resolution education. The result is a guide to conflict resolution education, published by the OJJDP in 1996, that is intended for schools and community organizations who serve juveniles. In the foreword to this guide, Reno joined with Secretary of Education Richard Riley to express the need for conflict resolution:

In this video developed for the Second Step program, students demonstrate conflict resolution through peer mediation.

No child should ever stay home from school because he or she is afraid. Too often, however, young people face conflicts either before, during, or after school. They are subjected to bullying, teasing, and senseless, sometimes fatal, disputes over clothing and other possessions. Many of these conflicts either begin at school, or they are brought into school from the home or the community. . . . We can intervene successfully to prevent conflicts from escalating into violent acts by providing young people with the knowledge and skills needed to settle disputes peacefully. Conflict resolution education can help bring about significant reductions in suspensions, disciplinary referrals, academic disruptions, playground fights, and family and sibling disputes.

These fourth and fifth graders in Brooklyn practice peer mediation in preparation for solving conflicts outside the classroom.

Learning conflict resolution is becoming a basic part of every young person's schooling. Schools alone cannot change a violent society, but they can teach alternatives to violence, teach how to act responsibly in social settings, and teach how to predict the consequences of behavior. These are the goals of conflict resolution education.

Some educators and criminologists, on the other hand, seem less hopeful. The most troubled schools where conflict resolution skills are badly needed, however, sometimes cannot implement these programs because they have burned-out personnel, lack competent leaders, and have poor attendance among staff and students. Conflict resolution education will not work if there is no one to teach it or if the students stay away.

Police partnerships with the community

Police departments across the country are developing partnerships with schools, parent groups, neighborhood associations, professional groups, businesses, service organizations, religious groups, and health professionals, who all share a common goal of eliminating and preventing teen violence. Now instead of acting independently, police are more likely to work with the community toward making the streets safe for long-term teen violence prevention programs to take root.

Police-community partnerships have two linked goals: to keep young people from being the victims of violence and to keep them from being the perpetrators of violence. The strategies for achieving these goals are based on bringing anticrime programs to educational and recreational segments of the community where they can help the most juveniles understand and resist violence.

For example, the Southeastern Michigan Spinal Cord Injury Center developed a unique partnership between police, schools, and victim groups. In this program, police accompany a group of young paraplegics and quadriplegics, all victims of gun violence, as they visit schools where they discuss, through personal example, what happens when guns are used to settle differences.

Often the police are instrumental in setting up a community partnership to reduce teen violence, but once the alliance is running, the police take a back seat. An example of such a partnership is Florida's Dade County Youth Crime Watch. Following a year in which the Florida public school system was shaken by 137 gun incidents, police and

Dade County officials created a partnership program involving the school board, the National Center to Prevent Handgun Violence, the broadcast and print media, and a variety of local agencies. This partnership provides schools with a comprehensive violence prevention program for all students from kindergarten to twelfth grade, their parents, and their teachers.

Numerous other communities across the country have formed their own educational violence prevention partnerships. The means of conducting these educational programs are as varied as the communities, but some of the more common ways of influencing teens and their families are through school assemblies, youth-led community projects, healthy living fairs, job fairs, television and newspaper campaigns, youth volunteer opportunities, expanded afterschool athletic and tutoring programs, anger management and conflict resolution courses for teens and parents, and the creation of drug-free and gun-free zones in schools and parks.

Successful partnerships

The Department of Justice examined a large number of partnering programs and found that the successful ones had three traits in common. First, the members of the partnership never began by assuming they knew exactly what was causing the community's teen violence; they sought to understand the problems from the viewpoints of residents, youth, police, and other members of the community. Second, they selected one or more strategies designed to eliminate the problems or their causes, and then they brought in as many people and organizations from the community as possible to help in carrying out the strategy. And third, the young people were always given meaningful roles and a real voice in all the efforts to end teen violence.

Preventing teen violence is obviously an important priority in America. Schools, police, businesses, service and religious organizations, the Department of Justice, Attorney General Janet Reno, the surgeon general, and President

Clinton are all involved. Although their efforts are communitywide, the most visible focal point is gang violence.

Preventing gang violence

Suppressing gangs through the use of tactical police actions is expensive. Identifying, locating, and arresting gang members occupies large numbers of police and consumes other law enforcement resources. The Department of Justice's OJJDP has concluded that these operations are successful in reducing gang violence, but only in a limited area and for as little as a few months before the gang activities return to the previous levels. As a result of the lack of success in suppressing gang violence, more communities are turning their energies to reducing the reasons kids turn to gangs in the first place.

The founders of Santa Cruz's Barrios Unidos, the members of the Community Build organization in South Central L.A., violence activist Luis J. Rodriguez, and many

An outreach volunteer educates peers about the dangers of teen violence and other issues.

other people who work directly with gang members have taken the position that gang-related violence is not the underlying problem but rather a symptom of the real problems. According to these experts, the real problems are the lack of meaningful jobs, poverty, dysfunctional families, police attitudes, and the despair and anger these things cause in the young people of the community.

In several respects, gangs provide teens with alternative ways of achieving status and success that are not available by legitimate means in the community. Now more communities are striving to provide the legitimate paths to success for potential and active gang members and those returning from incarceration by providing remedial education, training, career development, apprenticeships, and jobs.

L.A. Bridges

L.A. Bridges is one of a new crop of superprojects designed to prevent violence by providing legitimate alternatives for inner-city teens. L.A. Bridges, which began as a reaction to the gang slaying of a three-year-old girl, is an ambitious program designed to deter kids from joining gangs by using a coordinated group of strategies aimed at middle school youth. Strategies include reaching out to kids already caught up in gangs, conflict resolution education, job training, leadership training, and counseling on how to safely get out of gang life.

Beginning in 1997 with an $11.3 million grant from the city of Los Angeles, this program supports a number of established nonprofit agencies in their work with twelve- to fifteen-year-old youth in some of the city's highest crime areas. Juveniles in that age group are targeted because they are considered by authorities to be the most at risk for recruitment into gangs. The program also works with gang members who are trying to get out of gang life and the teens' families and schools.

Unlike previous antigang efforts, L.A. Bridges requires the groups and agencies it supports to demonstrate that their programs are achieving results in reducing gang violence in order to continue receiving funding. In the past, critics were concerned that the money given to many groups was wasted on activities that accomplished little or nothing to reduce the criminal activities of gangs. With the L.A. Bridges program, the results claimed by each group will have to be evaluated by an outside expert before continued funding is approved by the city.

Barrios Unidos

Some communities are choosing to embrace their gangs rather than wipe them out. That is not the same as saying they embrace violence and criminal activities. The idea is to draw gang members into constructive roles within their communities without requiring them to leave their gangs. One such organization that is using this approach is Barrios Unidos based in Santa Cruz, California.

Barrios Unidos, which is Spanish for united neighborhoods, provides a different kind of school for unemployed kids, gang members, and dropouts. Their school works on developing leadership and self-esteem with classes, job training, and community activities that reflect the cultures of the people they serve. The staff works with gang members and their parents to encourage positive attitude changes in individuals who have been living aggressive and violent lives.

The stated mission of Barrios Unidos is to prevent and reduce violence among youth by providing them with healthy alternatives. Barrios Unidos has a staff of teachers, counselors, and outreach workers, mostly people who have themselves faced and overcome the challenges facing teens in areas of high gang activity.

From their headquarters in a former furniture store, Barrios Unidos offers classes in computers, English, history, Spanish, video production, dance, art, writing, and silk screening. They also have a community outreach program that goes to schools, juvenile detention centers, and local neighborhoods to urge at-risk youth and their families to take advantage of Barrios Unidos programs. Their outreach program organizes multicultural discussions,

A gang member paints graffiti on a Los Angeles building. Scenes like this may become a thing of the past as more teens learn to take pride in their communities with the help of crime prevention outreach programs.

conflict resolution training, and cultural events that honor the diverse traditions within the community. The organization also provides jobs in a self-supporting silk screening plant where the teens learn business, design, production, and marketing skills.

Violence prevention radio

Among recent developments in community-level work to prevent gang violence are radio call-in shows featuring gang-savvy counselors on the microphone. The premier example is the radio program called Street Soldiers on KMEL-FM, a top San Francisco music station. The broadcast features counselors from the Omega Boys' Club, a club that serves teens and young adults with a four-pronged approach: peer counseling for incarcerated youths, academic help, job training, and violence prevention counseling on the radio.

KMEL-FM started Street Soldiers in 1991 with rapper M. C. Hammer, and though Hammer has left, the format remains the same. Teens call up the show and, without revealing their identities, talk on the air about anger, fear, and the violence they face.

Sometimes preventing violence by radio has immediate results. In 1994 a Samoan teenager was killed in a drive-by shooting, apparently by Filipino gang members. The phones at the radio station rang for weeks with calls from Samoans seeking revenge. One night the dead boy's father called the show to say he could not tolerate any more bloodshed. The revenge calls ended, and there was no attempt at retaliation.

Omega counselor Jack Jacqua describes the radio show as more than just a way to stop violence: "It is sort of a beacon of hope, a ray of sunshine. It says someone is actively, actually trying to do something about these conditions."

"Something to say yes to"

In his 1994 State of the Union address, President Clinton said:

> I urge you to consider this: As you demand tougher penalties for those who choose violence, let us also remember how we came to this sad point. . . . We have seen a stunning breakdown of community, family, and work. This has created a vast vacuum which has been filled by violence and drugs and gangs. So I ask you to remember that even as we say no to crime, we must give people, especially our young people, something to say yes to.

The problem of teen violence is one of the most tragic events in modern urban society. Civilized people have always believed that the future is in the children, and with the immense united efforts that are under way on so many levels, perhaps most of today's children will not only escape violence, but eventually live in a world where teen violence is a thing of the past. As Attorney General Janet Reno said to the National Forum on Preventing Crime and Violence in 1993, "Prevention is not a police, social worker, or prosecutor's function. It is everyone's function."

Glossary

adjudication: A judicial determination (judgment) that a juvenile is a delinquent offender, giving the court the power to pass sentence on the youth.

assault: Unlawful intentional infliction, or attempted or threatened infliction of less than serious bodily injury without a deadly or dangerous weapon. Aggravated assault is assault with a deadly weapon. Simple assault is not often distinctly named in statutes because it consists of all assaults not explicitly named and defined as serious.

cocaine: An illegal stimulant derived from the South American coca plant and consumed by sniffing, injecting, or smoking.

crack: A potent form of cocaine that is smoked as small chunks or "rocks."

delinquency offense: An act committed by a juvenile that if committed by an adult would require prosecution in a criminal court. Because the offense is committed by a juvenile, it falls within the jurisdiction of the juvenile court. Delinquent acts include crimes against persons, crimes against property, drug offenses, and crimes against public order.

disposition: The process in which a judge decides what will be done with an accused juvenile. Disposition may be dismissal, referral to foster care or other social agency, probation, placement in a special institution for juvenile offenders, or transfer to adult court.

homicide: Causing the death of another person without legal justification or excuse. The definition includes intentionally killing someone without legal justification or accidentally killing someone as a consequence of reckless or grossly negligent conduct. It includes all conduct encompassed by the terms murder, nonnegligent (voluntary) manslaughter, negligent (involuntary) manslaughter, and vehicular manslaughter.

juvenile: Youth at or below the upper age of juvenile court jurisdiction. This varies from state to state, below eighteen years of age in most states, but below seventeen, sixteen, or fifteen in some states.

juvenile delinquency: Behavior by an individual under the age of eighteen that is beyond parental control and therefore subject to legal action.

manslaughter: The unplanned yet unlawful killing of a person.

parole: The release of a prisoner before completion of the full time of sentence under the condition that no new crime be committed and certain other conditions be met.

pathological: Mentally or physically abnormal as a result of disease.

penal: Relating to punishment.

probation: Similar to parole, but it stands in lieu of incarceration.

probation officers: Individuals appointed by the courts to supervise offenders who have been released on probation.

rape: Sexual intercourse or attempted sexual intercourse with a female against her will by force or threat of force. Some states have enacted gender-neutral rape or sexual assault statutes that prohibit forced sexual penetration of either sex.

robbery: Unlawful taking or attempted taking of property that is in the immediate possession of another by force or threat of force.

Organizations to Contact

Boys and Girls Clubs of America
National Headquarters
1230 W. Peachtree Street NW
Atlanta, GA 30309-3447
(404)815-5700

National nonprofit, nongovernment organization providing youth development activities to more than 2 million youth between the ages of six and eighteen. Five regional headquarters, 1,976 facilities in all fifty states, Puerto Rico, and the Virgin Islands. Includes 320 facilities in public housing developments. Some clubs involved in intensive services to gang-involved youth.

Centers for Disease Control and Prevention
National Center for Injury Prevention and Control
1600 Clifton Rd. NE
Atlanta, GA 30333
(404)639-3311

Established in 1992 to improve American health by preventing premature death and disability caused by nonoccupational injury. Addresses youth violence, suicide, and family and intimate violence.

Committee for Children
2203 Airport Way South, Suite 500
Seattle, WA 98134-2027
(800)634-4449

Provides educational materials, original research, training, and community education for the prevention of child abuse and youth violence.

Covenant House
(800)999-9999

A free referral service to the nearest social agency for juveniles in trouble or for their families who need help.

Girls Incorporated
30 East 33rd St.
New York, NY 10016-5394
(212)689-3700

Committed to helping girls become strong, smart, and bold. Girls 6–18. Programs at almost 750 sites nationwide. Adolescent pregnancy prevention, gang violence intervention, academic encouragement.

Milton S. Eisenhower Foundation
1660 L Street NW, Suite 200
Washington, DC 20036
(202)429-0440
fax: (202)452-0169

Dedicated to reducing crime in inner-city neighborhoods through community programs, this foundation supports funding for programs like Head Start and Jobs Corps in the belief that better education and job opportunities will reduce juvenile crime and violence.

National Committee to Prevent Child Abuse
332 S. Michigan Ave., Suite 1600
Chicago, IL 60604-4357
(312)663-3520

Dedicated to preventing child abuse in all forms with programs in all fifty states.

National Council on Crime and Delinquency (NCCD)
685 Market St., Suite 620
San Francisco, CA 94105
(415)896-6223
fax: (415)896-5109

In existence for nearly a century, this is a nonprofit organization comprised of corrections specialists interested in the juvenile justice system, the prevention of crime, and fair, humane, effective, and economically sound approaches to crime control. It opposes putting minors in jail with adults.

National Crime Prevention Council (NCPC)
1700 K St. NW, 2nd Floor
Washington, DC 20006-3817
(202)466-6272
fax: (202)296-1356

NCPC advocates job training and other programs to reduce youth crime and violence, and provides training and technical assistance to groups interested in crime prevention.

National Criminal Justice Association (NCJA)
444 N. Capitol St. NW, Suite 618
Washington, DC 20001
(202)624-1440

Association of police chiefs, judges, and lawyers seeking to improve the states' administration of criminal and juvenile justice programs.

National Domestic Violence Hotline
(800)799-7233

Provides advice on all forms of family and dating abuse, anonymously, twenty-four hours a day. There is no charge to calling party and call record does not show up on phone bill.

National School Safety Center (NSSC)
4165 Thousand Oaks Blvd., Suite 290
Westlake Village, CA 91362
(805)373-9977
fax: (805)373-9277

A research organization that believes teacher training can help reduce school crime and violence.

U.S. Office of Juvenile Justice and Delinquency Prevention (OJJDP)
PO Box 6000
Rockville, MD 20849-6000
(800)851-3420
fax: (301)251-5212
e-mail: askncjrs@ncjrs.org
Internet: http://www.ncjrs.org/ojjhome.htm

This is the primary federal agency charged with monitoring and improving the juvenile justice system, and developing and funding programs whose goals are the prevention and control of illegal drug use and serious juvenile crime including youth gangs. It is a division of the Department of Justice.

Suggestions for Further Reading

Charles Patrick Ewing, *Kids Who Kill.* Lexington, MA: Lexington Books, 1990.

C. Ronald Huff, *Gangs in America.* Newbury Park, CA: Sage, 1990.

Rita Kramer, *At a Tender Age: Violent Youth and Juvenile Violence.* New York: Holt, Rinehart & Winston, 1988.

Darly Sander, *Focus on Teens in Trouble.* Santa Barbara, CA: ABC-CLIO, 1991.

Sanyika Shakur, *Monster: The Autobiography of an L.A. Gang Member.* New York: Grove/Atlantic Monthly Press, 1993.

Works Consulted

Elijah Anderson, "The Code of the Streets," *Atlantic Monthly,* May 1994.

Michael D. Biskup and Charles P. Cozic, eds., *Youth Violence.* San Diego: Greenhaven Press, 1992.

California Department of Youth Authority, *Selective Incapacitation and the Serious Offender,* by R. A. Haapanein. Sacramento, 1988.

Richard Cervantes, ed., *Substance Abuse and Gang Violence.* Newbury Park, CA: Sage, 1994.

Coalition for Juvenile Justice, *No Easy Answers: Juvenile Justice in a Climate of Fear,* Washington DC: Coalition for Juvenile Justice, 1995.

Stephen M. Cox and John J. Conrad, *Juvenile Justice: A Guide to Practice and Theory.* 4th ed. Brown & Benchmark, 1996.

Charles P. Cozic, ed., *Gangs.* San Diego: Greenhaven Press, 1996.

Allan Creighton and Paul Kivel, *Helping Teens Stop Violence: A Practical Guide for Counselors, Educators, and Parents.* Los Angeles: Hunter House, 1992.

N. Davidson, "Life Without Father," *National Policy Review,* 51:40–44, 1990.

Russell Eisenman, "The Young Desperadoes," *USA Today,* January 1994.

C. R. Fenwick, "Juvenile Court Intake Decision Making: The Importance of Family Affiliation," *Journal of Criminal Justice,* 10:443–53, 1982.

Todd Gitlin, "Imagebusters." *American Prospect,* Winter 1994.

Malcolm Gladwell, "Damaged: Why Do Some People Turn into Violent Criminals? New Evidence Suggests That It May All Be in the Brain," *New Yorker,* February 24, 1997.

Ellen Heath Grinney, *Delinquency and Criminal Behavior.* New York: Chelsea House, 1992.

David Hassamyer, "Armed Without a Conscience: Handguns Fuel Teen Violence," *San Diego Union-Tribune,* September 29, 1996.

Malcolm W. Klein, *The American Street Gang: Its Nature, Prevalence, and Control.* New York: Oxford University Press, 1995.

Robert Lichter et al., "New Studies on Sex and Violence on Television," *Phi Delta Kappan Magazine,* October 1995.

A. Miranda, *Gringo Justice.* South Bend, IN: University of Notre Dame Press, 1987.

Chris Morris, "Retailer Takes Lyrics Monitoring into Own Hands," *Billboard,* July 29, 1995.

National Council on Crime and Delinquency, *Images and Reality—Juvenile Crime, Youth Violence, and Public Policy,* by Michael Jones and Barry Krisberg. San Francisco, 1994.

Carla Peterson, "Windows to the World," *San Diego Union-Tribune,* September 29, 1996.

Gina Sikes, "Girls in the 'Hood," *Scholastic Update,* February 11, 1994.

C. E. Simonsen, *Juvenile Justice in America.* 2nd ed. New York: Macmillan, 1991.

Ruth H. Terrell, *A Kid's Guide to How to Stop the Violence.* New York: Avon, 1992.

U.S. Department of Health and Human Services, National Center on Child Abuse and Neglect, *Third National Incidence Study of Child Abuse and Neglect (NIS-3),* by Andrea Sedlak and Diane Broadhurst. Washington, DC: Government Printing Office, 1996.

U.S. Department of Justice, Office of Juvenile Justice and Delinquency Prevention, *Conflict Resolution Education: A Guide to Implementing Programs in Schools, Youth-Serving Organizations, and Community and Juvenile Justice Settings,* by Donna Crawford and Richard Bodine. Washington, DC: Government Printing Office, 1996.

U.S. Department of Justice, Office of Juvenile Justice and Delinquency Prevention, *Juvenile Justice Clearinghouse Fact Sheets.* Washington, DC: Government Printing Office, 1994.

U.S. Department of Justice, Office of Juvenile Justice and Delinquency Prevention, *Juvenile Offenders and Victims: A National Report,* by H. Snyder and M. Sickmund. Washington, DC: Government Printing Office, 1995.

U.S. Department of Justice, Office of Juvenile Justice and Delinquency Prevention, *State Responses to Serious and Violent Juvenile Crime Research Report,* by Shay Bilchik et al. Washington, DC: Government Printing Office, 1996.

U.S. Department of Justice, Office of Juvenile Justice and Delinquency Prevention, *Survey of Youth Gang Problems and Programs in 45 Cities and 6 States,* by I. A. Spergel et al. Washington DC: Government Printing Office, 1989.

U.S. Department of Justice, Office of Juvenile Justice and Delinquency Prevention, *Violent Families and Youth Violence Fact Sheet,* by Terence P. Thornberry. Washington, DC: Government Printing Office, 1994.

Judith Wallerstein and J. B. Kelly, *Surviving the Breakup.* New York: Basic Books, 1980.

Index

Picture Credits

About the Author

William Goodwin is a 1967 graduate of the University of California at Los Angeles; he has undertaken graduate study in biochemistry, education, and English. Since 1992 he has worked as a freelance writer, speaker, and consultant specializing in management, youth, industrial, and marine topics. He has also taught high school sciences, owned and operated a sailing school, written scripts for educational videos, and built a forty-three-foot boat. He shares a home in San Diego with his two teenagers, Gideon and Marilyn, and a very friendly bird named Pepper.